Inclusion for Children
with Speech and Language
Impairments

Accessing the Curriculum
and Promoting Personal
and Social Development

**Kate Ripley, Jenny Barrett
and Pam Fleming**

With illustrations by Jeremy Long

David Fulton Publishers
London

David Fulton Publishers Ltd
Ormond House, 26–27 Boswell Street, London WC1N 3JZ

www.fultonpublishers.co.uk

First published in Great Britain by David Fulton Publishers 2001

Note: The right of Kate Ripley, Jenny Barrett and Pam Fleming to be identified as the authors of this work has been asserted by them in accordance with the Copyright, Designs and Patents Act 1988.

British Library Cataloguing in Publication Data
A catalogue record for this book is available from the British Library

ISBN 1–85346–729–4

The publishers would like to thank John Cox for copy-editing and Sheila Harding for proofreading this book.

Typeset by Textype, Typesetters, Cambridge
Printed in Great Britain by Bell and Bain Ltd, Glasgow

Contents

Acknowledgements

We are most grateful to the following friends and colleagues for their contributions and advice, and without whom this book would not have been possible.

Jeremy Long whose understanding of speech and language impairment, gained from teaching children in a Speech and Language Unit for eight years, is superbly demonstrated by his inimitable drawings for this book.
Regan Delf and the County Psychological Service of East Sussex.
Isobel Bassett, Manager of the Speech and Language Therapy Service, South Downs Health (NHS) Trust and the therapists in her team.
The teachers of East Sussex Local Education Authority and Brighton, Hove and Portslade Local Education Authority.
The parents and children with whom we have worked over the years.

Introduction

So much in daily life is taken for granted, especially the skill of understanding language and being able to communicate our thoughts, feelings and aspirations. When this skill fails to develop, or is impaired by accident or injury, the result is often great anguish, despair and frustration. Speech and language impairment is devastating at any time in life, but for children it is particularly damaging, for it disrupts every aspect of their lives – their learning, their self-esteem, their relationships with others.

Language impairment is often a hidden handicap. Unlike other disabilities, there is nothing to show, no damaged arm or leg to engender sympathy and understanding. But it is one which can impact upon social development and access to the National Curriculum through all four of the key stages. The National Survey of children in Year 2 which was carried out in 1995 (Conti-Ramsden and Botting 1999a) suggested that only one per cent of the estimated five per cent of children with a specific language impairment were, at that age, identified on special needs registers in mainstream schools or receiving alternative provision.

Children who have problems with speech production, usually because of either limited control of the articulatory apparatus or problems with their sound system; phonological problems, are most likely to be identified in the early years. They may enter school with a history of intervention by the Speech and Language Therapy team which will alert their teachers to the possibilities of other difficulties with understanding or expressing themselves and to the risk of finding a phonic approach to literacy very hard.

The research would indicate, however, that four per cent of children with specific language impairment do not have their primary need recognised early in their educational career. They may subsequently appear on SEN registers with a range of labels which often include dyslexia, moderate learning difficulties, emotional behavioural difficulties and even autistic spectrum disorder.

Specific language impairment is not an homogenous disorder and the term may be used to describe a range of different language profiles. There have been many attempts to define specific language impairment to describe these profiles, which have met with varying degrees of success. There are still many areas of debate among researchers such as in the domain of semantic disorders, pragmatic disorders, semantic-pragmatic disorders and Asperger's Syndrome. These academic debates are not always helpful to the practitioners who are concerned with meeting the educational needs of the children.

In this book the terms specific language impairment, language impairment, and language disorder are used to describe the same condition, since all three terms are in common usage.

With a prevalence within the population of five to seven per cent, specific language impairment has a high incidence and should, therefore, be recognised as one of the most significant areas of special educational need. Spoken language is the main medium for instruction, explanation and discussion in the classroom and the language that is used becomes more abstract and decontextualised as children proceed through the education system. The language which is used as a medium for teaching and learning is very different from the language of social communication. The language which is used for conversation or on the playground is usually informal and context specific so that the actual words may carry only five per cent of the meaning. The language of the classroom involves a more precise knowledge of grammar and word meaning which develops over time. Children with a specific language impairment may have difficulties at the level of social communication and even more problems with the use of the abstract decontextualised style. They are, therefore, significantly disadvantaged in terms of access to the curriculum unless they are supported appropriately.

In this book we hope to:

- explain the range of language needs which may occur in the guise of a specific language impairment;
- help teachers in all key stages to identify children who may have a specific language impairment;
- suggest ways to support children with SLI in the classroom with reference to specific curriculum areas;
- explore how the needs of the children and the intervention strategies may change as the children proceed through the education system;
- review the implications for social inclusion and suggest ways of promoting this.

Chapter 1

The language system and how it develops

Man is a social animal. Social interaction and social communication are fundamental to normal development. The skills which are used for interaction and communication are complex, sophisticated and take many years to reach an adult level of competence.

To be an effective communicator the individual needs to develop an ability to understand what others say, receptive language, and a command of spoken language, expressive skills. Receptive and expressive language skills depend upon developing a knowledge of the sounds of a language (phonology), how meaning is attached to the specific sound patterns which we know as words (semantics) and the rules for how words are combined to make units of meaning (grammar). These language skills must then be used in a socially aware, flexible way which has regard for the needs of the partner in any exchange (pragmatics). All the elements of language are to some extent

Introduction

interdependent so that difficulties in any one area would be expected to have repercussions throughout the language system. The language system was represented graphically by Bloom and Lahey (1978) and this model is very useful when considering how language develops and understanding the needs of children who experience a specific language impairment (see Figure 1.1).

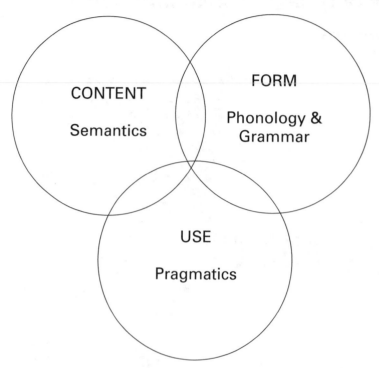

Figure 1.1

In the model, the phonology (sound system) and grammar of the language are described as the **form** of language, while the semantics, the meaning element, is described as the **content** of language and the pragmatic aspects of language are described as language in **use**. For children with a specific language impairment, development of the form and/or the content of language may be delayed or disordered so that understanding, **receptive** skills, and/or **expressive** skills may be affected.

Difficulties with form and content can and do affect how language is used, because what a child is able to understand or say will affect how they attempt to communicate with other people. It may take careful investigation to identify whether the apparent pragmatic problems are linked to difficulties with form and content, or to other factors.

To become an effective communicator it is also necessary to have an awareness of the interests, motives and possible intentions of other people. This ability to look at events and ideas from the perspective of another person has been called 'Theory of Mind' (Frith 1989) and it is this aspect of language which is a core problem for many people on the autistic spectrum. The form of their language (phonology and grammar) and even the content of their language may appear to be intact but they experience problems with using language in order to communicate effectively.

Examples

The impact of difficulties with Form and Content on language use

- An inability to make oneself understood may influence what one attempts to say and with whom one chooses to communicate. Thus, a child with an articulation problem may continue to use two-word phrases to everyone except close family who are able to understand his/her speech. Alternatively, frustrations about being unable to communicate effectively may precipitate behaviour problems.
- A failure to understand fully what is said, may result in some unexpected responses to questions. For example:

    Q: 'Where is your brother?' R: 'Phillip.'
    or
    Q: 'How are you?'   R: 'Me five.'

Alternatively, there may be a reluctance to try to engage in an interaction or a determination to steer the conversation to a safe known subject.

Language development

Newly born babies are able to demonstrate an amazing range of social interaction and communication skills so that in normally developing infants:

- a preference for faces over objects is evident at a few hours old;
- two-way interactions can be observed at two hours old (Snow 1972); These mark the beginning of coordinated turn-taking in what are known as proto-conversations;
- by eight weeks babies will respond differently to the sound of their own language and by four months they are able to distinguish their language from others which are quite similar, e.g. Spanish and Catalan:

    Just as bees learn fast to distinguish flowers from, say balloons or bus stops, so human children are pre-set by nature to pick out natural language sounds: they don't get distracted by barking dogs or quacking ducks' (Professor Jean Aitchison 1996 Reith Lecture, 'The Language Web');

- by six months babies will babble using language-like sounds and will produce single words by one year;
- in the first six months infants will react differently according to voice tone and facial expression;
- by six months there is evidence of 'theory of mind' when they look to a familiar adult for cues if they are uncertain about how to react to a new object or experience; this demonstrates that they anticipate that the other person will have a response to the situation which is independent of their own experience.

During their second year children show an explosion of naming words and start putting words together in a way which suggests some pre-programming of grammar. By the age of five most children will have mastered the basic aspects of the form of language and have an ability to understand language which is embedded in a real-life context. Early language develops most successfully, in a social context with parents or carers interacting in a dynamic way with their infants, so that they adapt the form and content of the language they use to match the developmental level of the child. The television or the video is no substitute for this process. For most children **Basic Interpersonal Communication Skills** (BICS) will be well established by the time a child enters school. However, as children progress through the education system the language demands become more complex and decontextualised so that children need to develop **Cognitive Academic Language Proficiency** (CALP) in order to access the language used in the classroom. Children with speech and language impairment usually need extra support in order to progress to this stage of language development.

Social skills and the social use of language are an even more complex set of skills and will continue to develop into adult life. Each new social situation which a person encounters requires new skills to be learned or established skills to be adapted. In turn, the ability to communicate affects the social experiences to which an individual is exposed and the success of their social interactions. These will have consequences for the development of the self-concept, positive self-esteem and behaviour patterns.

A successful communicator will gradually develop a range of skills which are summarised below:

- an awareness of the sound system of the language and the ability to use that system efficiently;
- an understanding and an ability to use the rules of grammar, including the function of different forms of utterance, e.g. question forms;
- a knowledge of the meaning of a wide range of words and the ability to choose the appropriate words to express what they want to communicate;
- an awareness that language is a tool with which to communicate with others and the motivation to initiate and respond to communication;
- an ability to manage the process of communication which requires the cooperation of the participants, e.g. to time turn-taking, to explore shared reference and to respond to the messages which are implied in, for example, tone, stress or intonation patterns;
- an awareness of the subtleties of communication so that the style of the utterance matches the context in which it takes place, e.g. not shouting a 'secret' across the room or greeting a teacher using the same style as to a close friend.

When children come into school they will be in the process of developing many of these skills but most children will show a range of language expertise by the age of five.

Language levels expected at 5 years

Speech

Intelligible under most conditions.
Immaturities may persist:

   – 'r', 'th'
   – consonant blends, particularly clusters e.g. 'str' insecure
    or reduced, e.g.   sh ⟶ s
                cg ⟶ sh
                st ⟶ d

Attention control

The child is at the integrated stage so that he/she is able to continue with an activity and listen to simple instructions. This may break down if the activity (e.g. tying a shoelace) or the instruction, is complex for that child.

Comprehension

Able to understand classroom instructions, particularly in context:

- to answer questions about past and future events
- to understand some abstract concepts
- to show some metacognitive features, e.g. jokes which play on words.

Expression

Able to:

- use complete sentences without omitting functions words
- join simple sentences using conjunctions, e.g. 'because'
- explain a sequence of events from his/her own experience.

Immaturities of syntax, e.g. irregular past tenses and plurals are still quite common.

Pragmatics

Able to:

- take turns in conversations
- adapt to the listener's needs in conversation.

Children should also be able to use language for a range of purposes:

- expression of feelings, needs and wants
- commenting and directing
- social greetings
- use of language in play
- response to and maintenance of conversation
- use of questioning
- use of descriptive language
- reporting previous experience
- reasoning
- prediction of events.

These early language goals are towards the development of **Basic Interpersonal Communication Skills** (BICS). Children in school need to develop **Cognitive Academic Language Proficiency** (CALP):

- the rules for exchanges are different
- words take on precise meanings
- language becomes more abstract
- language becomes less embedded in context.

Language impairment

For some children the development of language and social communication does not go according to plan. They may experience:

- delayed language development: language is slow to develop but it does follow the normal sequence and pattern of development;
- language disorder: language is delayed but also develops in an idiosyncratic, atypical way; for example
    - the sound system is restricted because the child does not understand the rules of how sounds are organised into words
    - understanding of language is well in advance of the ability to use words to communicate
    - understanding of language is extremely restricted and often impacts on the way in which a child expresses him/herself;
- articulation problems when the speech mechanisms do not work well so that they are difficult to understand.

Further definitions of the terminology which is commonly used when discussing language are presented in Appendix I.

Subsequent chapters of this book explore some of the difficulties which children who have impaired language development experience and how they may be supported in their personal, social and academic development.

Children who are unable to communicate effectively through language or to use language as a basis for further learning are handicapped socially, educationally and, as a consequence, emotionally.

(Byers-Brown and Edwards 1989)

The incidence of speech and language impairment

Many teachers, including experienced infant teachers, believe that the numbers of children who experience speech and language difficulties form an increasing percentage among the group of children who are identified as having special educational needs. The research evidence about the numbers of children affected is confusing because the criteria used for the identification of speech and language impairment varies between research studies. The picture is further complicated because:

- some children are slow to pass early milestones but then catch up (Paul 1991);
- the pattern of impairment can change with age (Bishop 1994);
- the overt language handicap may resolve over time but underlying impairments which affect academic progress can be identified using appropriate assessments well into Key Stage 3 (Bishop *et al.* 1996).

Webster and McConnell (1987) estimated that two or three children in every classroom were affected to a greater or lesser extent by language problems. Also speech and language therapists are finding that this is reflected in the increasing number of children either referred or still needing speech and language therapy at school age. The report from the Nuffield Project 1999 (Conti-Ramsden and Botting 1999a) indicated an incidence of speech and language impairment at about five per cent in Year 2. There is a higher incidence during the early years but 'natural' recovery is taking place during this time.

Bishop (1994) suggests that 40 per cent of the speech and language problems which are identified at four years are resolved by half-way through the fifth year. This 'natural recovery' rate appears to flatten after about six years so that 33 per cent at five years and only 10 per cent by seven years will improve without intervention.

The confusion about numbers reflects not only variations in the criteria which are used to assess speech and language impairment, but also the range of difficulties which speech and language impairment may encompass. Some speech and language impairments, for example, severe phonological problems, are only too obvious to anyone who attempts to interact with a child, whereas the more subtle semantic or comprehension problems may go undetected within the education system for a disturbingly long time.

Language is a complex interactive system and a child may experience difficulties in one or more parts of the system, for example phonology or semantics. Problems in any one part of the system will usually have implications for functioning in other parts of the system. Some areas of difficulty are more frequently found in association, for example phonological and grammatical problems, or semantic and lexical problems. However, problems with receptive language will invariably affect expressive language and language problems will interact with other aspects of development so that children with phonological problems are at high risk of literacy difficulties, and children with a range of language problems are at risk of social, emotional, or behavioural difficulties.

The main components of language are illustrated in Figure 1.2.

The language system

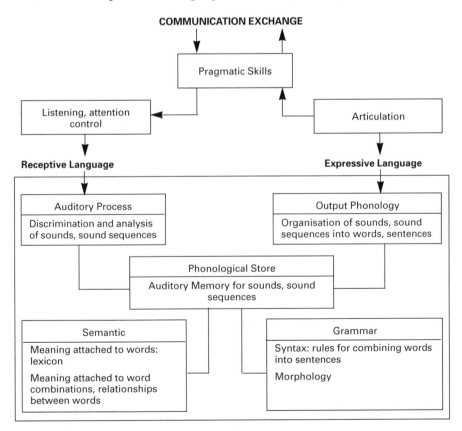

Figure 1.2

The components of the language system

Listening skills and attention control

Children who experience hearing or receptive language problems may present with limited auditory attention and immature listening skills. The information from medical investigators should establish whether a significant hearing loss is implicated in an individual case although the impact of fluctuating hearing losses on the development of language skills, particularly the sound system, is often underestimated.

Children with language disorders frequently show age-appropriate attention control for non-verbal tasks, including non-verbal tests of ability, but have poor attention for the auditory channel.

They may present as restless during story time, unable to follow instructions and find it hard to sustain auditory attention over time.

In view of the high level profile of Attention Deficit Disorder and Attention Deficit Hyperactivity Disorder, it is important to attempt to distinguish the individual who presents as highly distractible/hyperkinetic in a range of social and learning situations from the language impaired child who may show appropriate levels of attention control for non-verbal tasks and activities.

As with many other skills, attention control shows a clear pattern of development and children who have general developmental delay would be expected to show the pattern of attention control commensurate with their developmental age. The stages of the development of attention control were first described by Reynell (1976) and are still accepted today (see Figure 1.4). If a child is suspected of having a specific language impairment it will be important to consider their level of attention control for activities which do not involve listening skills as these children are at risk for a misdiagnosis of AD/HD (see Figure 1.3).

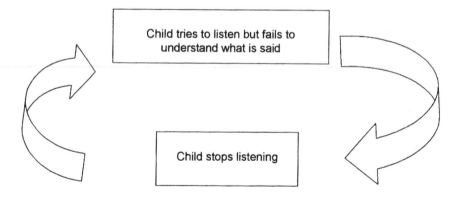

Figure 1.3

Auditory memory

Children who have immature listening skills and limited attention control for information presented in the auditory mode will experience difficulties with the retention of information that they hear if there is no visual support or hands-on experience as back up. These problems may be compounded by an immature sound system, phonological problems, weak auditory discrimination skills and receptive problems which may limit the network of meaning which can be triggered by any verbal message.

Assessment using informal or standardised tests may indicate that visual and kinaesthetic memory are the stronger modes and suggest that these can be used more effectively in teaching and learning.

Phonology

Typically, children with phonological problems know what they want to say, but their speech is difficult to understand. They use a small number of speech sounds (phonemes) to do the work of the 40 speech sounds used in English.

Stages in the development of attention control

Stage 1
Attention held momentarily by whatever is the dominant stimulus in the environment. Any new stimulus attracts attention: auditory/visual stimuli most noticeable sources of distraction.
Distractibility: the first year of life

Stage 2
The infant will concentrate for short periods of time on an activity which he/she has chosen. This is single channel attention so that verbal mediation or adult intervention are seen as intrusive.
Single channel attention: 1–2 years

Stage 3
Single channel attention persists but it becomes more flexible so that it is possible to shift from the activity to verbal directions which relate to the task and back again. An adult must ensure that attention (visual and auditory) is engaged before giving directions. Child can only assimilate directions if attention is focused on the source from which they come.
Single channel with flexibility: 2–3 years

Stage 4
A child is able to exercise more voluntary control over attention focusing but auditory stimuli in particular may be distracting. A visual focus on the speaker is still important for more complex instructions.
Attention focus under voluntary control: 3–4 years

Stage 5
A child is able to assimilate verbal instructions related to an activity in which he/she is engaged without needing to interrupt the task and look at the speaker. This two-channel attention integrates the auditory and visual aspects of learning.
Integrated attention possible for short periods: 5–6 years

Stage 6
Integrated attention is well established and can be sustained under voluntary control. It is possible to perform efficiently in a group/class situation because of the ability to process auditory information while engaged on a task or to focus on a task when surrounded by other sources of stimulation.
Integrated attention

Figure 1.4

They have not yet learned or are having difficulty learning the rules of how sounds are organised in words in order to convey meaning. For example:

- that there are a specific number of sequences of consonants (**c**'s) and vowels (**v**'s) which encompass all knowns words in our language. We do not have **ccccc** as they might in the Russian language, but we do have **ccvc** (spoon) or **cvcc** (wasp)
- that words are made up of smaller sound-string elements called syllables which are clearly identifiable and finite in number
- that by changing or contrasting speech sounds you can change the meaning of words '**b**ad'/'**d**ad'.

These children, whose phonological knowledge is poor and who use a restricted number of sounds in their speech are often described as having a 'phonological disability'. Such difficulties appear to have no physical cause and are considered to be associated with a linguistic problem.

Some children may not be able to produce certain sounds because of articulatory difficulties. They appear to experience problems with making and sequencing all the small rapid and accurate movements needed to produce articulate speech. The term used to describe their problems is **Developmental verbal dyspraxia** (DVD). Children with phonological disability are frequently much easier to decode because their speech sound patterns are more predictable; they may:

use 'front' sounds for 'back' sounds, e.g. 'tea' for 'key', 'tar' for 'car'
use explosive sounds for hissy sounds, e.g. 'dea' for 'sea'
miss off final consonant sounds in words, e.g. 'cu' for 'cup'.

Children with DVD however are frequently very unpredictable in what sounds they might produce and so on one occasion might say 'tea' for 'key' and on the next 'fi' for 'key'. It is possible for children to have both articulatory and phonological problems and need support in both areas.

Grammar

Phonological and grammatical errors tend to occur together in some children's spoken language, since both are associated with learning the rules of the linguistic system, i.e. the rules of phonology and the rules of grammar. Children with grammatical problems often make false starts, pause and struggle to produce the right structure. They tend to string information-bearing words together, omitting function words, e.g. 'Daddy car' rather than 'Daddy is in the car'. Spoken language also lacks many of the features that mark verb tense, plurals and possession, e.g. /pt/ in 'help<u>ed</u>' and /ts/ in 'ca<u>ts</u>' and girl's as in 'the girl's bag'. Many children with expressive grammatical problems are also impaired in their understanding of grammatical structures, e.g. the passive form of a verb (e.g. the boy was pushed by the girl) or negation (e.g. don't). This can lead to misunderstandings as when 'Don't go out now' is processed as 'Go out now' and acted upon.

Semantic

Semantics involve:

- the meaning of words and concepts:
  - children first learn labels for objects, people and other things which are part of their everyday experience. Understanding the meaning of some other

words may involve a gradual evolution over time so that the meaning becomes more precise and in line with adult usage. For example, 'boat' may be first applied to one plastic boat in the bath. The meaning applied to the word may then extend to all objects that float. (Technically speaking, the semantic field for that word has then become over-extended whereas it was previously under-extended.) Gradually the child will learn to apply the word 'boat' to a specific class of object; the semantic field for the word will have been brought in line with common adult usage. Children with speech and language impairment may struggle to reach this stage of development for a wide range of words, particularly concept words.

- the relationships between words which facilitates the understanding of:
  - causation – 'John walked into the tree because he was looking at the aeroplane'
  - hierarchical ordering, e.g. the concept words, examples of categories and items in the categories (see Figure 1.5)
  - contrasts, e.g. big – little
  - how context may affect meaning (I built a lego <u>model</u>/The <u>model</u> tripped on the catwalk
  - the agent of an action, e.g. John gave the book to Mary – Mary gave the book to John.

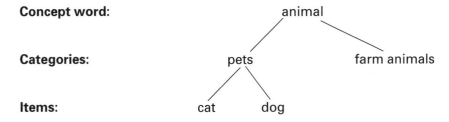

Concept word: animal

Categories: pets   farm animals

Items: cat   dog

Figure 1.5

Children with semantic problems usually begin to speak late, but their speech is then relatively clear and fluent. For the most part their speech sounds 'alright' and any misunderstanding or inaccuracy in word meaning is overlooked or ascribed to an aspect of a child's behaviour. 'He's a bit idiosyncratic in the way he chooses his words' (parent). These children may have problems with the meaning of language in whatever medium it is presented – spoken, signed or written.

Problems with precise word meaning and understanding the relationships between words may affect the understanding of grammatically complex sentences. This may result in children responding to one or two key words in a sentence rather than to the meaning of the entire sentence. As a consequence of this incomplete language processing, answers may appear to be 'odd' and off-target, e.g:

Q: 'Who did you go shopping with (at the weekend)?'
R: 'New shoes.'

The lexicon

Many children who are language-impaired have difficulty in naming familiar objects, this is often called a 'word-finding problem'. They take longer to learn new words, and may be slow to name objects in pictures when sharing a book. They may also perform poorly in 'naming' vocabulary tasks. Sometimes the problem extends to other classes of words, most typically verbs and adjectives.

The smaller the class of words the better the chance of recall.

There are several possible causes for a word-finding problem which might include:

- erratic listening which has affected the acquisition of word meanings and the words may be stored inaccurately;
- a word may have been established in the lexicon but there is a problem with accessing the stored information; this 'tip of the tongue' phenomenon may happen to anyone at times and can become frustratingly more frequent with ageing;
- a weak sound system which may make it hard to recognise the sound patterns which make up a word and, therefore, to attach meaning to these;
- a problem in linking the meaning to the sound patterns of words.

Word learning and word recognition involve the phonological system, the lexicon and an understanding of semantics (word meaning), as shown in Figure 1.6. If a child has difficulties with this process in the oral mode (spoken language), they will be at risk for similar problems with the written mode (literacy).

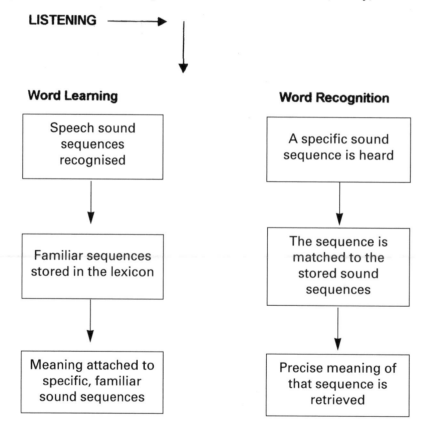

Figure 1.6 Word Learning and Word Recognition

Possible problems

- Problems retaining in memory sequences of speech sounds
- Problems attaching meaning to sequences of speech sounds: making the link
- Problems with presentations of meaning: semantic boundaries unclear

Pragmatics

Children with pragmatic problems have difficulty using language in a social context. In the Figure 1.2 pragmatics are at the interface between the two partners in a conversational exchange. For children on the autistic spectrum difficulties with pragmatics often appear to be at the core of their problems with language, so they may seem unaware of the needs of their conversational partner because of 'theory of mind' issues. They do not seem to understand the social rules of:

- turn-taking in conversation;
- the conventions for joining and ending an exchange;
- topic maintenance and shared meaning;
- the amount of information which it may be assumed that the other person knows already;
- how to repair a conversation which has broken down.

Children with language impairment may also show some of these problems at a behavioural level. However, they do not originate from a lack of 'theory of mind' but rather from the difficulties which having restricted language skills impose upon any social interaction. For example:

- a child who experiences articulation problems may appear to be a reluctant communicator and not turn take in conversation because they do not expect their contribution to be understood;
- the same child may just walk away if the person they are is talking to has not understood what they have said rather than attempt to repair the conversation; alternatively, they may continue to use two-word phrases to everyone except close family members who are able to understand their speech;
- a child who has difficulties with receptive language may not follow what is being asked of them and do or say the 'wrong' thing which may make them behaviour appear 'odd' or 'naughty': for example,

    T: 'After you have cleared away, you can go out to play.'
    Child's response – heads for the door because only the most recent part of the sentence has been processed;

- a child with semantic problems may not process the whole message from the teacher and respond out of context to key words or phrases which he recognises; this off-target responding may mirror the autistic problem with topic maintenance.

Difficulties with semantics and pragmatics are often linked and Rapin and Allen (1987) described a Semantic-Pragmatic Disorder in Children. There is still debate about whether a Semantic-Pragmatic Disorder equates with high functioning autism and the term is certainly still used as a euphemism for autism by some practitioners. It is important to recognise within the context of a discussion about language impairment that semantic disorders do exist in the absence of pragmatic problems other than those which are directly associated with the faulty processing of language meaning as illustrated above. Children who have good skills of social interaction are often able to disguise their semantic difficulties until they begin to fail academically.

Case Study

A girl was only identified as having significant semantic problems when she was referred to the educational psychologist for exam concessions in Year 11. She was attractive and had a real talent in art and music but was perceived as a quiet, shy girl who was reluctant to talk to adults ('a bit sulky'). Significantly, she had moved secondary school because of verbal bullying and it was clear that she did not have the language competence to defend herself in the cut and thrust of teenage verbal repartee. Her family, close friends and boyfriend were aware that they needed to simplify the language that they used with her but she had given up asking teachers if she did not understand because she still did not follow what they had said on the second or third repetition. Fortunately, most children are identified at an earlier stage in their educational career, usually when problems with reading comprehension become apparent.

Chapter 2

Multidisciplinary assessment

The assessment of speech and language difficulties is based upon a range of underlying theoretical models which structure the way in which different professionals think about speech and language.

Four approaches are outlined below. The first three are used largely by therapists and the fourth is used mainly in education. All of them are important and together they can produce a balanced perspective while using only one approach can be very limiting.

It is important to understand these different perspectives because if teachers and therapists are to work well together they need to understand that there are differences in the way in which professionals from other backgrounds think about speech and language. The differences come about through their respective professional training and philosophy. When the differences are appreciated, the strengths of both can be employed to their greatest advantage.

The assessment of speech and language

Medical approaches

Medical Model
• Causes
• Symptoms
• Diagnosis
• Intervention

Figure 2.1

The traditional medical approach to speech and language difficulties, which has been influential over the years, is to offer an explanation in terms of 'causes' and 'symptoms' (see Figure 2.1). A 'diagnosis' which identifies and names the problems is considered to be important and this will then suggest particular measures which might be taken. This approach is appropriate when it is possible to identify a cause for the language impairment such as an ear infection or there is a structural problem such as a cleft lip or palate or there are difficulties with movement of the oral apparatus, i.e. tongue, lips, jaw, soft palate or breathing. However, it is difficult to 'label' many speech and language problems in this way and so a comprehensive description cannot be drawn from using this model alone since it cannot throw light upon the interactive aspects of language or on the impact that the difficulties have upon the child's social and emotional development and learning. For this to be achieved additional information is required about the nature of the difficulties such as might be offered by the linguistic model.

Linguistic models

The emphasis of this approach which has been developing over the last 25 years is on giving a detailed description of the form, i.e. grammar and phonology; content, i.e. meanings and the function of language using models such as the one by Bloom and Lahey (1978 Chapter 1). This description can then give rise to the precise identification of a child's speech and language difficulties which can inform therapy and teaching. While it fulfils its aims in facilitating details and descriptions of problematic areas of language, it should be remembered that difficulties seldom fall into neat categories and that each area listed above depends upon the other two areas of the language system in order to operate successfully.

Psycholinguistic and cognitive approaches

Another approach, which is seen as being extremely useful by speech and language therapists and educational psychologists, is based upon how language is processed. Using a variety of task materials, aspects of visual and auditory processing skills and movement coordination are carefully analysed. It is then possible to consider issues around language 'input' and

Language can be viewed in three dimensions:

CONTENT
FORM
USE

These components interact at different levels.

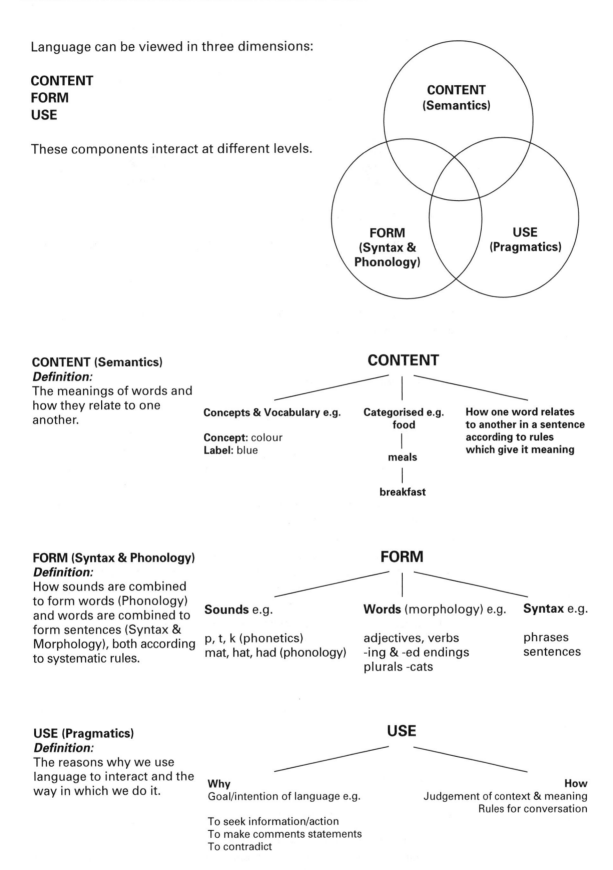

CONTENT (Semantics)
Definition:
The meanings of words and how they relate to one another.

CONTENT

Concepts & Vocabulary e.g.

Concept: colour
Label: blue

Categorised e.g. food
|
meals
|
breakfast

How one word relates to another in a sentence according to rules which give it meaning

FORM (Syntax & Phonology)
Definition:
How sounds are combined to form words (Phonology) and words are combined to form sentences (Syntax & Morphology), both according to systematic rules.

FORM

Sounds e.g.

p, t, k (phonetics)
mat, hat, had (phonology)

Words (morphology) e.g.

adjectives, verbs
-ing & -ed endings
plurals -cats

Syntax e.g.

phrases
sentences

USE (Pragmatics)
Definition:
The reasons why we use language to interact and the way in which we do it.

USE

Why
Goal/intention of language e.g.

To seek information/action
To make comments statements
To contradict

How
Judgement of context & meaning
Rules for conversation

Figure 2.2

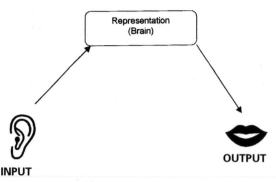

Figure 2.3 Psycholinguistic model

'output': where 'input' corresponds to receptive language and 'output' to expressive language. Using this approach a much clearer idea can be gained of the particular points at which difficulties are occurring in pupils who might otherwise appear to present as having very similar speech or language problems. It is also possible, using this model, to identify strengths to draw upon for teaching and therapy.

Educational approaches

In contrast to the above approaches which are used predominantly by speech and language therapists, the National Curriculum attainment target of 'Speaking and listening' exemplifies how language is viewed in an educational setting. In 'Speaking and listening' emphasis is placed upon communication as a *social process*. When a child's performance is giving cause for concern teachers might typically explore interest, motivation, situational knowledge, emotional status and the powers of concentration of the child. Another aspect of language investigation in the educational setting is an examination of the language of the classroom. It is necessary to question whether the teacher's language can be understood and whether the language content of a particular curriculum area, with the wealth of potential for confusion, is creating difficulties for the child. More will be said of this later.

Contributions to the assessment of speech and language difficulties can be made by speech and language therapists, teachers and educational psychologists, each possibly providing information from different perspectives and theoretical models. However, if these are understood the result is a rich qualitative description which can inform the planning of teaching and therapy for the pupil with speech and/or language difficulties. We now turn to the contribution made by each of these professionals.

Assessment by teachers

Assessment by the class teacher

Assessment by the class teacher, including observation, is an important contribution to the overall assessment of children's speech and language development. The particular value of the teacher's assessment lies in the opportunity for observation of a child in their natural surroundings. Often speech and language therapists comment that such observations reveal areas of strength or difficulty which have previously gone unnoticed as well as providing further data in support of the therapist's assessment.

Teachers can make contributions to an assessment by gathering examples of the pupil's receptive and expressive language and particularly of the way in which the pupils communicate with their peers. Observation in relation to language comprehension can be made by noting the pupil's behaviour in response to the teacher's instructions. The pupil might for example show evidence of misunderstandings, make unrelated remarks, seek verbal or non-verbal assistance, appear to 'disobey' or to fall out with peers for no apparent reason. All these behaviours might suggest that the child is failing to understand. To return however to a point made earlier, pupils' difficulties can be exacerbated by the language of the classroom; therefore an important part of the assessment will be for the teacher to reflect upon his/her own language as part of the delivery of the curriculum and the creation of the 'language environment'.

Teachers can also usefully collect data concerning pupils' spoken language. Despite the fact that it is felt by many teachers that they are ill equipped to make judgements about pupils' expressive language, they can nevertheless make useful contributions concerning, for example, accuracy in producing sounds, vocabulary levels, the ability to find words and to produce the correct word order.

The classroom setting is also ideal for observing the pupil with pragmatic difficulties, i.e. with using language for a range of purposes. Behaviours which are indicative of pragmatic difficulties are poor turn-taking in conversation, giving and gaining attention, repairing the conversation, i.e. asking for and giving clarification and, more generally, using language and behaving appropriately in terms of the activity being undertaken.

Assessment by the SENCO

In the last section, it was noted that assessment in the classroom is not only about looking at the pupil's difficulties but also considering the language of the classroom. It is therefore an extremely worthwhile exercise to arrange for the SENCO or a support teacher to observe the pupil within the classroom setting and to feed back to the teacher.

In these circumstances the observer may well wish to make a note of the teacher's behaviour when giving instructions and information, watching, for example, whether information is presented in a verbal or non-verbal form.

Observation of the child's overall behaviour in response to the teacher is also illuminating. For example, does the pupil show evidence of grasping the topic or the point of the activity? Does he/she appear to 'disobey' or fail to carry out instructions? Does the child start the activity late and begin by watching what the others are doing? Consideration should also be made of the teacher's response to the pupil. For example, is adequate time given for a response? Is the pupil allowed flexibility in the way he/she shows under-standing, e.g. by using key words, diagrams, cartoon drawings, gesture, computer work?

Useful references and resources

AFASIC checklists
Teaching Talking (Anne Locke 1985)
British Picture Vocabulary Scales (BPVS) (check first whether or not a speech and language therapist has done this assessment) (Dunn *et al.* 1997)
Boehm Test of Basic Concepts (Boehm 1988)
Profiles of Development (Webster and Webster 1990)
Classroom Observation Schedule (Daines *et al.* 1996)

The **AFASIC checklists** give an overview of the child's strengths and weaknesses and provide an indication as to whether intervention is required from the speech and language therapist. If teachers have the time to undertake other assessments as suggested, these will provide a more detailed picture of the child's functioning.

Teaching Talking: a good overview of stages of development of children's language development for preschool/early years, Key Stage 1 and Key Stage 2, then identifies the detailed profile to use with the child, divided into physical skills, understanding and expressive skills.

The **British Picture Vocabulary Scales** (BPVS) assesses a child's understanding of single words (3–18 years).

Boehm Test of Basic Concepts: using a series of pictures, this assesses a child's understanding of key basic concepts needed for learning at Key Stage 1.

Profiles of Development provide a developmental sequence and a means by which evidence can be collected in the number of key areas of development in order to make teaching plans and report on children's progress.

Observation Guide: a classroom observation schedule to use with children who may have speech and language difficulties (*Spotlight on SEN Speech and Language Difficulties*, Daines *et al.* 1996).

Assessment by the speech and language therapist

The broad aims for assessment by a speech and language therapist working within the educational framework are the same as those for colleagues who work with children who have other kinds of complex needs. They are:

- to identify the need for intervention;
- to determine the child/client's strengths and weaknesses;
- to determine the severity of the problem;
- to enable the management plans to be made.

Ideally, the assessment of a school age child is a joint undertaking by the therapist, parent(s)/carer(s) and teacher(s) since a child's language can vary according to context. The actual process of assessment can vary slightly depending on where the assessment is carried out. In a school, the therapist will have the benefit of observing the child in class using language for different activities, but may not have access to the range of assessment materials which would be available at the local clinic. Once the child is in school, communication with staff is seen as essential in order to obtain the teacher's perception of the nature of the child's speech and language difficulty.

The speech and language therapist, as well as using a whole range of procedures to gain an insight into the nature and complexity of the child's linguistic difficulties, also needs the insights of parents and teacher in order to have a complete overview of the problems.

Summary of Assessment Procedure

Figure 2.4 outlines the main elements of the assessment procedure which would usually involve formal and informal assessments together with observation of the child in a range of interactions.

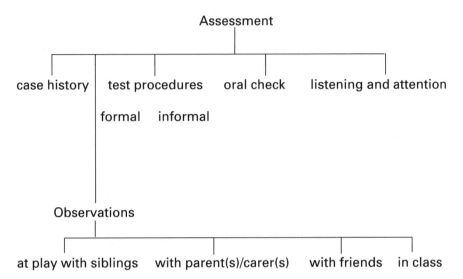

Figure 2.4

Referral

Prior to assessment, a referral needs to be made. Sometimes teachers express concern regarding whether or not to refer a child for a speech and language therapy assessment. The majority of children are referred for assessment at the preschool stage by health visitors who identify children with special needs through the various developmental checks they carry out. However, occasionally, for a variety of reasons, e.g. no attendance for a developmental check, children with speech and language impairment reach school without having been seen by a speech and language therapist. There are some excellent checklists available for teachers to use which give clear guidelines as to whether referral is needed or not (e.g. the AFASIC checklists). Therapists would always advise a referral if there is any doubt about the child's speech, language or communication development. Speech and language therapists currently operate an open referral system and take referrals from many different agencies, professionals and other individuals as shown in Figure 2.5.

Case history

The first task for the speech and language therapist is to take a detailed case history, regardless of any other information which has been made available in the referral documents. In a case history, the following areas will be covered with most of the information being provided by the parents/carers.

Pregnancy and birth
Feeding
Speech and language development
Other milestones – crawling; sitting; walking; when clean/dry
(age and order in which these occurred)
Hearing
Health history
Vision
Attention and listening
Socialisation of child
Behaviour – frustration; relating to the world; likes/dislikes; how challenging or otherwise, e.g. withdrawn; any obsessions
Coordination
Family history (if any)
Family details, e.g. number and age of siblings; parent(s) occupation(s)
Educational progress.

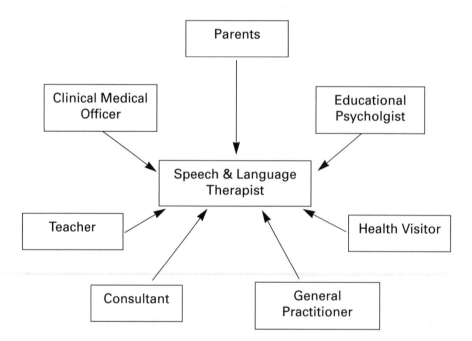

Figure 2.5 Referral routes to Speech and Language Therapist

Test procedures

Speech and language therapists use a whole range of published assessments (see Appendix 2). Some of these assessments may be 'formal', that is they give scores for various aspects of language development. In order to do this, the tests have been standardised on a large number of children and can give, therefore, an indication how a child is functioning in relation to his/her peers. Other assessments are 'informal' and these include profiling procedures, observational schedules and interviews, as well as the therapist's own observations of the child's speech, language and communication. There are many such procedures which cover all aspects of communicative behaviour, and some involve the cooperation of parents and teachers. Using both formal and informal assessment procedures, speech and language therapists will gather detailed information on:

symbolic understanding
receptive language skills
expressive language skills
use of language: pragmatics
phonology/articulation
voice quality, e.g. hoarse
fluency
prosody: aspects of communication which include intonation, pitch,
    rhythm, rate, volume
listening and attention
phonological awareness
communicative behaviour
oral skills: movement of the lips and tongue when speaking is not involved
feeding.

Oral skills

Some children experience difficulties with making and coordinating the fine and rapid movements needed to articulate sounds for speech. Frequently this is associated with problems in actually copying and/or making movements of the tongue, lips, jaw, soft palate and face, e.g. making the tongue move rapidly from side to side, elevating the tip, pursing lips. If therapists feel this is a specific problem for a child, they will check this aspect of oral functioning using a comprehensive checklist.

Feeding

Some children, particularly those who may have the condition known as oral/verbal dyspraxia, may be 'fussy' or 'faddy' eaters. Therapists would want to observe their feeding patterns with reference to the type, range and temperature of food tolerated by the child.

Listening and attention

Research shows that an increasing number of children entering school have poor listening and attention skills (Ward 1992). Some of these will also have speech and language difficulties and the speech and language therapist will assess these aspects of linguistic behaviour using various checklists. Attention skills develop following a clear developmental sequence and so it is possible to see the stage of development that a child has reached and start to support them to reach the next and successive stages. (Figure 2.3).

Observation

Observation is crucial to the whole process of assessment. Speech and language therapists learn a great deal from observing a child in different contexts, with different tasks and people.

Referring on

A speech and language therapist may decide, following assessment, that the child needs to be seen by other professional colleagues. Further assessment may be needed from:

an educational psychologist
a paediatrician or other consultant, e.g. ENT, consultant, plastic surgeon,

neurodevelopmental paediatrician
clinical psychologist/psychiatrist
audiologist
occupational therapist/physiotherapist
social services.

The speech and language therapist will never see a child unless there is full agreement from the parent(s)/carer(s). At all stages, parents/carers are involved in the assessment procedure.

Assessment by the educational psychologist

During the early years the educational psychologist would usually be asked to become involved with a child because health professionals were concerned about how the child's needs might be met in an educational setting. These preschool referrals will usually have detailed background information about early development and the results of assessments which have already been carried out by the paediatrician or by therapists such as the speech and language therapist. Once a child is in school, the educational psychologist may be the first 'outside agency' to become involved at the request of the school. Whether the referral is from the school, parent(s) or health professionals, the role of the educational psychologist is to work closely with parents, speech and language therapists and teachers in order to:

- clarify the nature of the speech and language problem;
- assess the implications for learning;
- assess the classroom as a learning environment for that child;
- assess the implications for access to the National Curriculum;
- identify the social, emotional, behavioural implications of the language impairment.

It is estimated that for about 50 per cent of children, their speech and language impairment will be associated with more global delay. In terms of planning appropriate language programmes and educational experiences, it is important to distinguish between this group and those individuals who experience specific speech and language impairment. Administration of non-verbal tests of abilities, such as the Snijders-Ooman, Kaufman or Leiter International Performance Scale may help to clarify the cognitive profile.

In the early years it may be difficult to distinguish children who have a specific speech and language disorder (SLI) from those who have a communication disorder and, therefore, are on the autistic spectrum. In particular, children with severe receptive problems may show anxiety in response to changes of routine because the verbal explanations which are intended to prepare them for change are not understood. They may also show limited imagination in their play. Typically, these features recede as their language skills develop, but it may require assessment of their response to an appropriate language programme over time to clarify the issue.

In other cases, a strong communicative intent and the skilled use of non-verbal means of communication will distinguish children, even with severe language impairment, from those on the autistic spectrum.

The focus of the assessment by the educational psychologist will be to ensure that the educational environment for the language impaired child is able to facilitate the learning needs of that child and to promote social and emotional development.

The assessment by the educational psychologist may involve:

- the collation of information which is already available, such as
  - developmental, medical and educational history
  - involvement with therapists and learning support services
  - the child's present level of functioning
  - the emotional reaction to the speech and language impairment and how this affects social relationships
  - the learning environment of the child, including the levels of support available
  - the child's response to the learning environment as indicated by attainments and rates of progress;
- observation of the child in a range of settings: at home; in class; on the playground;
- an assessment of the language profile and how this affects how the child responds in the classroom; for example, problems with listening skills may be implicated in restless behaviour during the literacy hour or limited language comprehension may affect the response to instructions;
- individual assessment of key areas of functioning which may include:
  - non-verbal abilities
  - motor-skills because of the high level of coincidence of speech and language impairment and motor impairment
  - literacy skills
  - social and emotional development.

The educational psychologist should, on the basis of this information, be able to advise about a range of issues, such as:

- the arrangements for the implementation of a language programme at school;
- the balance between individual work/group work within the language programme;
- the balance between structured teaching/language learning in context within the overall language programme;
- modifications to the delivery of the curriculum which would include how information is presented to the child;
- strategies to alleviate the associated difficulties with the development of literacy and numeracy skills;
- the development of social skills and social communication skills;
- the provision of alternative means of communication, such as signing, if appropriate.

Children with speech and language impairment will usually have complex needs and so it is only by considering the contributions from members of a multidisciplinary team that a reliable identification of their needs can be made. Some children may share superficial behavioural responses with other groups of children, for example those with AD/HD or who are on the autistic spectrum. It may, therefore, take careful observation and assessment over time to decide whether the primary difficulty is with speech and language. Parents and teachers who know the child well and have observed their response in a range of different situations are very important contributors to this multidisciplinary approach to assessment.

Chapter 3

Reading and the literacy hour

The literacy hour: Introduction

This chapter considers the impact of particular speech and language difficulties upon the acquisition of literacy skills. The strategies that are suggested can form the basis of individual teaching where this is possible. However, they can also be incorporated into the group activities that are part of the literacy hour, since it is anticipated that many children who do not have identified speech and language difficulties could also benefit.

Phonological awareness before literacy

Once young children have begun to develop listening skills, particularly sound discrimination, they become increasingly aware of how words can sound alike. They discover the pleasurable activity of making words 'rhyme' and can be heard 'playing' with rhymes, which can include non words with real words, e.g. 'thingy, wingy, singy, mingy'. Sometimes, they can be heard to change well-known nursery rhymes, e.g. 'Humpty, Wumpty sat on a ball; Humpty Wumpty had a great fall' etc. As the child matures, it becomes apparent, more explicit, that the connected speech sounds which make up spoken language can be broken into smaller parts or 'segments' and in time these segments can also be manipulated.

This set of skills, which children have already begun to develop before they enter school, are referred to as 'phonological awareness'. This term has fairly recently appeared in the lexicon of teachers, primarily as a result of the National Literacy Strategy. As long ago as 1983 and 1985, Bradley and Bryant, in their research established a link between the acquisition of early rhyming skills and the later successful development of reading. Subsequent studies by other researchers have supported this hypothesis (Goswami 1996, Blackman 1991, Layton *et al.* 1996). These skills are also instrumental in a child filing the word accurately in his/her lexicon; what is termed the 'phonological representation' of a word, and being able to retrieve that word as and when needed.

Phonological awareness involves a child/individual reflecting on the sound structure of an utterance rather than it's meaning (Stackhouse and Wells 1997).

In practice this refers to the set of skills that enable us to analyse the sounds in the words we say and hear:

- segmenting – that is dividing
  - sentences into words
  - words into syllables
  - words in phonemes;
- rhyme – recognising and discriminating words that sound similar
  - in nursery rhymes such as Jack and Jill went up the hill
  - in single words that 'rhyme', eg 'hat, mat, cat' or 'late, straight'.

So, before children can learn to read the skill of phonological awareness has begun to emerge and they demonstrate that certain aspects are easier to grasp at first and others more difficult. In spoken language, syllables are the easiest segments or 'bits' of the word to detect and children who are quite young will nod, clap, tap, out the syllable structure of words. They often start with their own names followed by the names of objects and individuals closest to them, e.g. name of dolly, teddy, brother, sister. This, the simplest of skills, could be described as the easiest 'level' of phonological awareness. The next level involves segmenting syllables into onset and rime ('onset' refers to any consonant which precedes the vowel and 'rime' that part of the syllable that includes the vowel sound and any consonants following it).

The third and most difficult level of phonological awareness is that of segmenting (breaking down) syllables into phonemes and a task most young children are incapable of doing successfully.

Levels of phonological awareness

Syllables: com/pu/ter; gi/raffe; rhi/no/ce/ros
Onsets and rimes: c/up; b/in; f/at
Phonemes: /s/; /u/; /n/;   /h/; /ou/; /se/

The two simpler levels of phonological awareness, syllables and onset and rime may well be easier to deal with as part of the more general skill of understanding and producing speech. The divisions between these respective segments of words are certainly more easily isolated acoustically, than individual phonemes. Even when phonemes are pronounced correctly (without the familiar intrusive 'schwa', e.g. *'per'* instead of 'p' which is a voiceless sound), they do not easily blend to sound like a word.

Children with speech and language difficulties frequently find the whole area of phonological awareness confusing. Those with poor phonology and/or oral verbal dyspraxia are most likely to have poor phonological awareness. They have not yet developed a clear understanding of how the speech and language sound system is organised, and are unable to easily make and sequence the fine and rapid movements needed to articulate language. It follows, therefore, they would be most unlikely to have a set of skills well developed which would enable them to analyse the sounds in words they say and hear.

The literacy hour

In this section the impact of a range of speech and language difficulties is considered, relating to the acquisition of skills at word, sentence and text level.

Literacy hour: Word level

(a) Word finding, i.e. retrieving learned vocabulary spoken and written:

  - at its most severe this can involve difficulty with the retrieval of letter sounds and names;
  - it often produces laboured reading because of problems retrieving key words, e.g. names and places.

(b) Difficulties with short-term auditory/verbal memory:

  - inhibits vocabulary developments;
  - prevents verbal rehearsal for:
    - initial sound/letter links which will remain insecure for longer
    - sound sequencing
    - sound blending
    - encoding of sounds for spelling.

(c) Difficulties with long-term verbal learning:

  - impacts on the retrieval of phonological information from long-term memory, e.g. letter/sound knowledge, nursery rhymes, personal information;
  - impacts on the more complex aspects of word learning, e.g. words with several meanings; this will affect subjects such as science where commonly used vocabulary has an alternative 'scientific' meaning.

(d) Difficulties with phonological awareness, i.e. the ability to reflect on the sound structure of words *in the absence of written letters*:

  - difficulties with discriminating syllables in words;
  - difficulties with discriminating sounds in words;
  - difficulties with discriminating sequences of sounds;

- difficulties with establishing grapheme/phoneme links;
- 'fuzzy' phonological representations of words and sounds in words will impact on spelling and word building via the grapheme/phoneme link; however, (see pages 80–1) using a 'Breakthrough to Literacy' approach can help to clarify word boundaries.

  These difficulties will make a phonic approach to reading difficult for children who have phonological problems. Expect slow progress in this area.

(e) Difficulties with words may result in a heavy reliance on visual clues:

- picture cues:
  - word meaning may be missed if pictures do not match the text
  - may divert attention from the written text
  - may always be the first point of reference;
- some easy reading books encourage a heavy reliance on picture cues which may detract attention from the text;
- a sight vocabulary approach is important to supplement weaker/ auditory phonological skills.

> *Strategies:* Teaching four concrete words (i.e. nouns/verbs) to one abstract word with a low network of meaning can help (e.g. when). Signs or symbols reinforce abstract word acquisition.

(f) Difficulties with receptive language may result in:

- slow acquisition of learning word meaning;
- a poor understanding of the metalanguage used in teaching, e.g. 'think', 'remember', 'forget', 'learn';
- confusion about relevant 'technical' vocabulary, e.g. 'word', 'sentence', 'phoneme';
- a slow acquisition of learning categorisation and concept words.

Children with speech and language impairment may need specific teaching of even common use vocabulary as well as metalinguistic terms, technical words, categorisation and concept words.

Literacy hour: Sentence level

(a) Difficulties with receptive grammar can lead to:

- loss of meaning as sentences become more complex, e.g. sentences of more than ten words, sentences with subordinate clauses;
- poor prediction of what class of word might come next in a sentence; for children with competent language this cuts down the field of search, e.g. 'the' is usually followed by a noun (e.g. 'the *cat*'), or a noun phrase is followed by a verb (e.g. 'the cat *sat*');
- a limited understanding of the key phrases upon which text comprehension depends, e.g.
  - the significance of word order: John kicked Ted/Ted kicked John
  - the passive form of a verb: John was kicked by Ted
  - the negative: John did not kick Ted.

(b) Difficulties with expressive grammar can lead to:

- an inability to generate sentences for writing.

> *Strategy:* A 'Breakthrough to Literacy' approach can be useful, especially if the word categories are colour coded.

- problems with prioritising and attaching meaning to morphology (e.g. plural versus possessive 's'), tense endings, pronouns; these may need to be specifically taught;
- word order problems which can confuse the listener and make it hard to generate meaningful sentences, e.g.

Q: 'When is your birthday?'
R: 'The November of 23rd month soon' (aged 8 years);

> *Strategy:* It is easier to work on this using the child's attempts at written language than to correct speech: if the teaching of grammatical structure is a target, modelling of the correct grammatical structure is the key strategy for spoken language.

- the substitution of words which are in the same broad category but are not entirely appropriate, e.g. letter/stamp/address/envelope used more or less arbitrarily in sentences. This reflects confused semantic boundaries and a lack of precision in word meaning, e.g.
  'He stuck the letter on to post it'
  'That shirt's got a dirty belt' (collar)
  'He banged his hands together' (clapped).

(c) Difficulties with language use, i.e. understanding and using language that is appropriate for the context can lead to:

- an inability to generate appropriate and salient sentences;
- poor understanding of the 'voice' of sentences which depends on the punctuation and the structure of the sentence, e.g. dialogue, description, question form;
- misunderstanding non-literal language such as idioms and metaphors may cause particular problems for children who have difficulties with word meaning.

Beyond word recognition to text comprehension

Literacy hour: Text level – younger students

(a) Difficulties with receptive language.
In the primary phase of education difficulties with language will affect literacy acquisition in the following ways:

- following simple instructions

> *Strategy:* These may need to be differentiated, modelled and cued visually.

- difficulties with discussion of text: off target responses may indicate that a few key words rather than the text meaning have been processed

> *Strategy:* Pre-preparation of text and key-wording may help.

● retelling stories

> *Strategy:* For strategies refer to speaking and listening (see p. 66).

● slow acquisition of familiar formats for writing or telling stories, e.g. 'once upon a time . . .'

> *Strategy:* Writing frames are helpful to develop these skills (see pp. 86–7).

● confusion due to problems distinguishing social language from knowledge language when texts are being discussed, e.g. did it really happen, was it a dream, or did he just hope it might happen?;
● difficulties arising from a mismatch between order of mention and order of action in texts

> *Strategy:* This can be clarified visually as picture sequences of flow charts.

(b) Difficulties with expressive language may

● Inhibit expression of views about text

> *Strategy:* Preparation individually or in a small group will support this activity in a class context; discussion of the ideas before the class lesson to include brainstorming/word association activities/word and phrase collection.

● cause children to have problems with the initiation of responses and, therefore, they will need to be allowed more time to respond without other children 'helping';
● inhibit the development of writing for different audiences;
● cause difficulties with generating notes for future reference;
● cause problems with sequencing events to retell stories;
● inhibits identification and understanding of rhyme, rhythm and other features of sound, particularly for poetry writing and poetry appreciation; children may need more practice with this at a simple level

> *Strategy:* Key wording a prepared test or practice at taking visual notes using icons.

Examples of visual notes using icons:
'The first thing I want you to do is to find a picture of the Golden Hind in a book. Then I want you to use this picture to make your own drawing of the Golden Hind on a sheet of paper. Use crayons to make your drawing (Figure 3.1a).

Next, get some glue and a mat from the cupboard next door.

Then get some scissors.

Cut round your drawing of the Golden Hind.

Then stick your ship somewhere on the sea on this poster on the wall (Figure 3.1b).'

Figure 3.1 Examples of visual notes using icons

List the things they were not told. What might they get 'wrong', or get stuck on?

(c) Difficulties with language use (i.e. understanding and using language appropriately for the context)

- affects full understanding of text, i.e. inhibits inference and comprehension of the voice of the text as carried by the structure (e.g. dialogue, prose, play script, poetry);
- affects prediction especially if the plot depends on the feelings and motivations of the characters

Strategy: Drama, role play, play scripts and the discussion of relevant picture materials may support this understanding.

- inhibits an appreciation of why particular words and phrases have been selected to make a particular impact;
- inhibits using language to discuss and reflect on language (meta-language): this becomes more significant as children move through the education system and more abstract and decontextualised language is used by teachers and expected from learners (see pp. 62–4);
- prevent identifying salience for text comprehension and in free writing;
- word-finding difficulties may impact upon retelling, discussing, predicting, describing, expressing news and sequencing events (see pp. 76–7).

Children who experience difficulties with the organisation of their spoken language will, inevitably, experience problems with 'free' writing. They may need extra support for this:

Strategy:
- present picture sequences for the child to match to a caption – the caption may have to be pre-prepared by the teacher, or support be given to the child to help them make up a title
- sample writing frame (see pp. 86–7)
- diagrams and illustrations to help sequence the plot.

Difficulties with comprehension of text for older pupils

> *We read to gain information and to be entertained. Reading is, therefore, about understanding, not about recognition.*   *(Yuill and Oakhill 1998)*

Many children who have speech and language problems associated with a sound system that has been slow to develop, or was disordered, will have difficulties with a phonic approach to reading and spelling and so make a slow start with literacy skills.

A longitudinal study which followed up children who had specific language difficulties identified preschool, showed that some of these children, the good outcome group, were reading at an age appropriate level by seven to eight years old (Conti-Ramsden and Botting 1999a). However, when even these children were reassessed in the early years at secondary school, they were found to have problems with text comprehension. Yuill and Oakhill (1998), in studies of reading comprehension, also found a group of children with the same type of problems who had not been identified as having speech and language difficulties in the early years. It is not unusual for language problems to go unnoticed in school unless speech is affected as such problems are all too easily attributed to shyness or non-cooperation (Hadley 1991). The incidence of this pattern of reading difficulty, which is sometimes called **hyperlexia**, is also high among verbal children with autistic spectrum disorders.

In order to understand a text, various skills are needed which include:

- understanding meaning at the level of single words, sentences and whole texts: the meaning of individual sentences needs to be integrated to understand paragraphs and paragraphs integrated to give the storyline some coherence;

- processing the language used in the sentences which would include; a knowledge of grammar so that the significance of features such as tense markers, negatives or plurals is recognised;
- a knowledge of linguistic concepts such as 'why . . . because', modifying clauses, the conditional;
- integrating the above skills in order to
  - identify main events of the plot
  - sequence the main events of the plot
  - get the main idea of a story
  - understand characters and their motivations
  - discuss cause and effect to give plot cohesion.

Children who have language problems are often slow to develop these subskills which are needed for the comprehension of a text. When asked to discuss what they have read they may show difficulties in a range of areas which may alert their teachers to underlying language problems. To understand a text children need to be able to:

- identify important versus irrelevant details, so that they can be prioritised accordingly;
- maintain comprehension monitoring so that misleading decoding errors can be corrected from the context;
- have the awareness that there may be a non-literal interpretation of the text;
- have the ability to look beyond the literal meaning of the text;
- understand inference from other parts of the text to comprehend the meaning of individual passages, e.g. 'tears rolling down her cheeks' might be associated with hilarity or sadness;
- understand texts for which the plot is dependent upon the feelings and emotions of the characters;
- identify fact from fiction;
- have an awareness and understanding of different styles of writing, e.g. poetic form, dialogue;
- have an awareness and understanding that texts may have difference purposes, e.g. advertisement.

First printed in The Times Educational Supplement

Yuill and Oakhill 1998 found that poor reading comprehenders had difficulties with inference, even when the text was available for reference so that the difficulties could not be accounted for by a memory problem. These children were also less likely to make inferences which connected different parts of a text and less likely to be able to infer the meaning of a word from its context. The children also had difficulties with comprehension monitoring so that they were poor at detecting inconsistencies in a short story.

Older children with limited reading comprehension may have additional problems with subjects and tasks which involve metalinguistic skills such as:

- the ability to understand context and probability: this involves an understanding of the environmental context, including the social situation, so that the likelihood of an event occurring or an ambiguity in the text can be analysed in terms of what is already known;
- the ability to understand metalanguage: understanding the rubic of questions, especially for examinations (e.g. compare and contrast): more practice with outline plans to ensure salience, relevance to the question and cohesion will be needed;
- the understanding of jokes and puns:
  - in structured forms of humour such as jokes and riddles, the punch-line frequently relies on breaking the linguistic expectations of the listener, e.g.
    'What do you get if you cross an elephant with a mouse?'
    'Large holes in the skirting board'
  - puns are 'plays' on words, e.g. a slogan used in advertising for a new kind of adhesive – 'Our word is your bond.'

Difficulties with reading comprehension may be the first clue that an older child also has problems with the comprehension of spoken language. It is not unusual for subsequent assessments to reveal that a child has hitherto undetected semantic difficulties.

Case Study 'Helen'

One That Got Away . . . Almost

Helen – a girl CA 8.08

Referral to Educational Psychology Services:
Slow progress with reading after two terms in a Junior School in a new authority.

Observations:

Strengths	– attractive
	– good non-verbal skills
	– positive relationship with peers
	– hard working and eager to please

Difficulties	– confused by verbal instructions
	– followed class routines by observing others
	– 'lost' in class discussions and verbal exchanges

Assessment
Receptive Grammar (TROG) Age Equivalent 5 years 0 months
British Picture Vocabulary Scales (BPVS) Age Equivalent 4 years 10 months

Outcome:
Assessment by the speech and language therapist
A language programme was delivered in school
Text was used to develop oral language skills

The suggestion arising from the work of Bishop and Edmundsen (1987) with children with SLI and the work of Yuill and Oakhill (1988) with poor comprehenders is depicted in Figure 3.2.

Poor reading comprehension

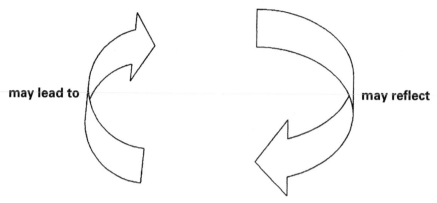

may lead to

may reflect

a specific language impairment:
often with semantics or with processing grammar

Figure 3.2

Strategies to support comprehension

The strategies which have been used to support reading comprehension can also be helpful for children who have difficulties with comprehension in the processing of spoken language. Unlike spoken language, which is transient, written language remains available and can be 'revisited' over time.

(a) **Text modifications**. This may involve making additions or changes to the text to make it more memorable. Strategies which are universally used include the use of titles, sub-headings, summaries, font changes, underlining or bold type. One diagram is 'worth a thousand words' remains good advice for those who are visualisers rather than having linguistic processing as their preferred cognitive style. Supplementing strategies such as the use of pic-symbols, icons, mind maps and drawn summaries can be helpful for children.

(b) **Working on the text**. This involves engaging in activities while reading or soon after reading a text. These might include note taking, key-wording, summarising, thinking about a title for each paragraph and then for the whole text.

(c) **Teaching processing strategies**. These can be taught by asking children key questions about the text in small groups. Once these have been practised, children can be encouraged to go through the process independently.
Does the text relate to anything that you know about already?
How does it relate to this previous knowledge?
Does it support or contradict what is already known?
How might any discrepancies be resolved?

(d) **Comprehension monitoring**. Children with SLI who learn to decode print quite effectively may, apparently, fail to self-correct errors which are inconsistent with the sentence context or the meaning of the sentence as a whole, e.g.: 'He went [down] the road to the shops and got the legs [eggs] for his mum brown.' Support to focus upon the meaning of the text may be needed and this can be achieved by talking about the text in a way that is similar to the techniques used for 'comprehension monitoring' of speech.

Yuill and Oakhill 1988 give an example of sentence work when the children were asked to discuss what they could say about a sentence or story from the individual words:

(Example 1) *'Sleepy Tom was late for school again'*

- 'Tom' suggests that we are talking about a boy rather than the teacher who would probably be 'Mr' in the sentence;
- in the context of the whole sentence 'again' may give a clue that this was happening quite often, so did he always stay up late?

This type of discussion would lead easily into inference – why did Tom often go to bed late?; and to prediction – what might happen to Tom when he got to school?

(e) **Inference training**. Some texts were selected by Yuill to focus on Inference training and the children were invited to discuss the answers to key questions.

(Example 2) *Billy was crying. His whole day was spoilt. All his work had been broken by the wave. His mother came to stop him crying, but she accidentally stepped on the only tower that was left. Billy cried even more.*
Questions: *Where was Billy?*
                Why was Billy crying?
                What had the wave broken?
                Why did Billy cry even more?

(f) **Imagery training**. For children and adults who find it hard to remember words, imagery training which uses the visual system to support remembering can be very helpful. Imagery can be encouraged by reading short stories to children and then showing them a series of pictures which represent the main sequence of events (about four in number) and a single picture depicting the main event. The stories and pictures are discussed and the children use the pictures to answer questions about the story.

Once the use of pictures is established, the children are encouraged to make their own pictures in their heads (which are real to them) about a story. These mental pictures are discussed in the group and the children answer questions about the story.

Imagery training was found to help all children to answer comprehension questions and children with poor reading comprehension showed the most significant gains in their performance.

Case Study

Chris had a long history of speech and language impairment; as a youngster he had spent 18 months in a Language Unit and had subsequently been supported by the Speech and Language Therapist throughout his school career. At 18 years of age he was preparing to take his A level geography. His teacher had only recently begun to understand the real nature of Chris' language difficulties, i.e. his problems with verbal comprehension and understanding of complex texts.

The following example shows how the teacher differentiated one of the course questions.

Agriculture

Study Figure 3.3, showing two sketches of possible lines of development in the Yorkshire Dales National Park.

(a)   (b)

Figure 3.3

(a) Evaluate the technique used as a means of communicating issues concerning agricultural development to the general public.

Teacher:	What is the question asking?
Chris:	Evaluate the technique, that's weighing up the two means of communication.
Teacher:	Do it.
Chris:	Between the two there are a lot of changes. Hedgerows have been taken out. Fields are bigger. There is reforestation. Also there is increased erosion due to more overland flow. There are new buildings.
Teacher:	Check you are still answering the question.
Chris:	I've started wrong, I'm confused about the first words. 'Technique', that's how something is done, or method.
Teacher:	Right – what technique is being used? What method, to communicate issues.
Chris:	(No answer)
Teacher:	Figures/text/photo/diagram?
Chris:	Photo.
Teacher:	No, look.
Chris:	Sketch.

Discussion continues:

Teacher:	Chris shows a clear picture of change from a basic approach (e.g. no machinery), but starts to get into detail on content again, I stop him and re-direct him by saying there's not enough information just in pictures, needs text, facts and figures to back it up, but constraint of usage of land does come over.)
Chris:	A looks more natural, B more false looking (see Figure 3.3).

With reference to *either* developed *or* less developed countries outline the measures farmers may adopt to overcome the physical constraints of their land (see Figure 3.4).

Teacher:	What are the key words?
Chris:	Developed or less developed.
Teacher:	Which one is for you?
Chris:	Developed.
Teacher:	Then?

Chris:	Measures farmers use to overcome physical constraints.
Teacher:	Tell the meaning of this in your own words.
Chris:	What farmers will do, methods they will use to overcome physical constraints e.g. a river in a field.
Teacher:	What is the meaning of 'constraint'?
Chris:	Something which will stop you doing something.
Teacher:	Yes but in this situation what does *physical* constraint mean?
Chris:	Features of the land itself e.g. hilly, position, soil, whether there are trees.
Teacher:	You're missing out on a whole area of 'physical' – you said the land itself – anything more than just land?
Chris:	Processes?
Teacher:	No, what about above the land.
Chris:	Pollution?
Teacher:	No (Teacher points out of of the window).
Chris:	Weather!
Teacher:	How can you set out/organise your notes on a page for answering the question in a way that will help ensure that you *do* answer the question?

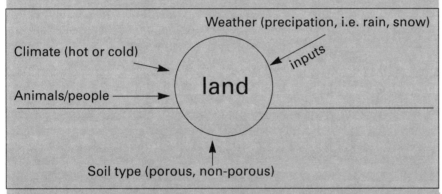

Figure 3.4

Teacher:	This sketch is a good approach to answering one part of the question. Which?
Chris:	The constraints.
Teacher:	What are you missing out?
Chris:	What farmers can do to over come these problems.
Teacher:	Show me how you can help yourself with this

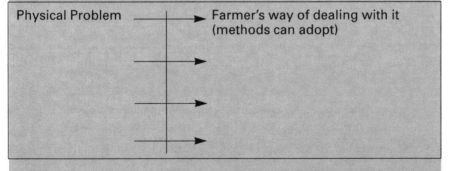

Figure 3.5

Chapter 4

The Numeracy Strategy

Stages in teaching children mathematical vocabulary

The majority of the vocabulary that is used in mathematics is first used in a social context, e.g. 'More' is initially learned as a way for an action to be repeated, 'More swing'. It is then learned as increasing mass or quantity (not numbered) as in 'More sand'. Finally, it is learned in relation to the number of items. Most of the words so precisely used in mathematics to refer to time, space and number begin their life by referring to characteristics of human action. Children need to be taught the extended meanings of these words before they are taught the number system or are expected to understand and use mathematical language.

When embarking upon the teaching of vocabulary, it is important to check the child's understanding of the word in a social context. If the child demonstrates no knowledge of the word in a social context, then he/she lacks the foundation for learning more complex terms. So, for example, the term 'middle' would probably be understood as something that mother has said meaning 'don't interrupt', e.g. 'I'm in the middle of making this cake . . . just a minute.' The next stage is the child's understanding of 'middle' when it relates to space, for example, the middle of a circle, the middle of a line and the middle of a small number of items. This is then followed by sequences in time: the middle one of three sounds, the middle one of three words, the middle one of three letter sounds. The final stage is numerical middle in which the child also needs to understand what the number represents.

The teaching sequence for terms such as 'middle', 'more', 'first', 'every', 'between', is as follows:

- begin by using the children themselves, e.g. first/middle in the line.
- use concrete objects such as toys which are representational and symbolic, e.g. bricks, cubes.
- finally, move to pictures which are two-dimensional visual representations.

As with the language of instruction in other areas of the curriculum, the language used in mathematics teaching can be more confusing to the children than the mathematical principle being taught. Table 4.1 below gives examples of the complex level of language which is required even in a Key Stage 2 Language Unit where the issues of vocabulary control are well understood.

Table 4.1

Language used in a maths session on 100s, 10s and units	
Counting	Ask which number it is
Counting on	What is it?
Does number get bigger?	Different person
Does number get smaller?	Different number
Another way	How many tens?
Number gets higher	How many units?
Count forward	How big the number is
Stop	Is she right?
Turn it over	Makes
Count on from that number	Put them together
Add some hundreds	What is it called?
Same for you	What have we got?
Turn over a card	Count three cubes

The tables that follow give examples of vocabulary taken from the National Numeracy Strategy for Key Stages 1 and 2 and has been classified according to ease of access for children with speech and language impairment. It is important to note that the introduction of new vocabulary in the National Numeracy Strategy does not follow the developmental sequence for language acquisition.

Table of Key Stage 1 and 2 Vocabulary

Table 4.2

Words and Concepts: Mathematical Vocabulary Yr R			
Subject	Concrete and, therefore, relatively easy vocabulary	Social use adapted to a more precise use	Abstract or metalanguage
(i) Counting	Number How many Count	None!	Number names (representative of items) None indicating nothingness
	Less (acquired developmentally much later than more, avoid teaching them altogether)	More Odd Even How many times Pattern Pair	Every, other
	?Guess	Close to	Nearly
		Just over Just under (not) enough Too many	About the same as Just over Just under (not) enough Too many Same number As many as
(ii) Comparing and ordering numbers		More Larger (refers to mass/number of items as well as size)	Fewer
		Smallest (refers to physical size)	Fewer
		Most Biggest Largest Greatest	
		Smallest	Fewest Least Compare Order Size (in reference to numbers) First After Second third last Last but one Before After
	Next	Next	Between

'More'	Social use refers to 'again' with the young child and 'mass' e.g. more sweets.
'Odd'	Social use refers to a person/thing who/that is unusual in the way he/she/it behaves, looks.
'Close to'	For social use with the young child this will be understood in the context of physical proximity, e.g. 'you're sitting too close to me!'.
'Just over'	An abstract concept: young children at this stage understand 'just over' in everyday usage as 'just over here/there' and not in relation to for example 'just over 10', in the numerical sense, which is a very abstract idea.
'Before/after'	Children understand these first in spatial and temporal terms not in the more abstract numerical sense (see p. 78 regarding teaching order in developmental sequence of vocabulary learning).
'None'	Refers to 'don't want none of that' in the social context and could also refer to a 'nun'.

Table 4.3

Words and Concepts: Mathematical Vocabulary Yr 1			
Subject	**Concrete and therefore relatively easy vocabulary**	**Social use adapted to a more precise use**	**Abstract or meta-language**
Instructions	Count Copy Arrow Colour Trace	Change Back Front Middle Ring	Think Imagine Remember Next to Opposite Apart Edge

'Change'	Social use refers to an action usually related to clothes, e.g. 'change your shoes/trousers/sweater'. Children may also have understood this in the context of 'where's the change?', referring to the money remaining after a shopping trip.
'Ring'	Social use refers to an item that you wear on your finger, or 'let's make a ring' meaning 'let's make a circle'.
'Think'	The abstract use here means 'to reflect upon' rather than 'I think this tastes nice' which is a more usual context for it to be used.
'Apart'	This will certainly be interpreted as 'a part' and understood in a very literal fashion.

Words and Concepts: Mathematical Vocabulary Year 2

Table 4.4

Words and Concepts: Mathematical Vocabulary Yr 2			
Subject	**Concrete and therefore relatively easy vocabulary**	**Social use adapted to a more precise use**	**Abstract or metalanguage**
Patterns and Symmetry	Size	Bigger Larger Smaller Reflection	Symmetrical repeating pattern
Time	Clock Now Quick/quickly	List Array (a ray) Round up How many times Watch	Soon Sequence Stands for Represents Roughly Halfway between Round down

'Bigger/larger'	Even at Year 2, children with speech and language impairment will most likely interpret these words in a literal fashion – so if the child is asked 'which number is larger, **2** or 3' he/she will answer '2' referring to its physical attributes, rather than it's numerical 'size'.
'Array'	This will certainly be understood as 'a ray' as in 'a ray of sunshine'.
'Stands for'	This will be interpreted as 'standing up for' since its abstract meaning 'represents' will not yet be understood by children with speech and language impairment.
'How many times'	This phrase is borrowed from the social context and frequently understood in a negative fashion, 'how many times do I have to tell you to go to bed?'

Table 4.5

Words and Concepts: Mathematical Vocabulary Yr 3			
Subject	**Concrete and therefore relatively easy vocabulary**	**Social use adapted to a more precise use**	**Abstract or metalanguage**
Making decisions and reasoning	Right Wrong Correct Answer	Operation Sign Puzzle	Method Different between Symbol Equation
Handling date	Count List	Axis Set Sort Table	Frequency table Most/least popular Most/least common
Instructions	Look at Point to Show me	Name Place Sketch Question	Predict Interpret Investigate
'Popular/common'	These two words may only be understood in a very context-bound way as they are frequently used to describe 'soap operas', e.g. 'that popular soap, Eastenders . . .', or used in them, e.g. 'she's as common as muck'.		
'Place'	This word is often understood in the context of 'that's a nice place to go to', rather than in its numerical context.		
'Predict'	Children with speech and language impairment find prediction of any kind problematical since this skill involves the use of language to 'think through' what might happen.		

Learning Number Names

Children may have a range of difficulties which inhibit the effective learning of number names. These include:

Phonological problems – a fuzzy representation of words can lead to the confusion of number names, e.g. thirteen/thirty. This would affect the understanding of place value, in addition to any problems with sequencing.

Visual cueing and experiential learning are helpful to establish these concepts.

Word-finding problems – there may be difficulties with the recall of number names or they may be confused, e.g. sixteen for sixty. Even when there is a good understanding of computational skills, children can appear to have difficulties because number names are temporarily lost or forgotten or because of memory limitations.

Maths, memory and understanding

Memory limitations and a weak understanding of the language of number may result in the following problems:

- Remembering number names in sequence. Counting on may be difficult to learn.
- Difficulties with any form of mental arithmetic because this requires holding information in working memory while performing mathematical operations.
- Remembering the process from day to day, e.g.
  - how to perform subtraction with a carrying figure
  - visual representation in the form of a flow diagram can support this
  - solving a problem which has more than one component
  - visual representation by means of flow diagrams.
- Developing flexible methods of working using language to mediate the problem-solving process, e.g. to add 19 and 39. The most efficient way would be $20 + 40 - 2$.
- When problems are written in words, decoding with understanding is needed so that the process which is required is recognised. This may be particularly confusing when different words are used to describe the same process, e.g.
  - add 1 and 2
  - what is the sum of 1 and 2
  - I have a sweet in one hand and two in the other, how many do I have all together?
  - What is the total number of sweets?
- Some problems are worded so that a knowledge of concepts such as cause and effects are assumed, e.g. in a classical maths 'filling the bath' problem, it has to be understood that the bath might overflow.
  Children with receptive language problems have difficulty with this as well as with any tasks which involve time concepts.
- A process which has been learned in one context may not be recognised as relevant in another context, e.g. recognising the need to use a knowledge of addition and subtraction acquired with unifix cubes in order to answer a question after a traffic survey:
  Q: How many cars did you see?
  Q: How many red cars did you see?

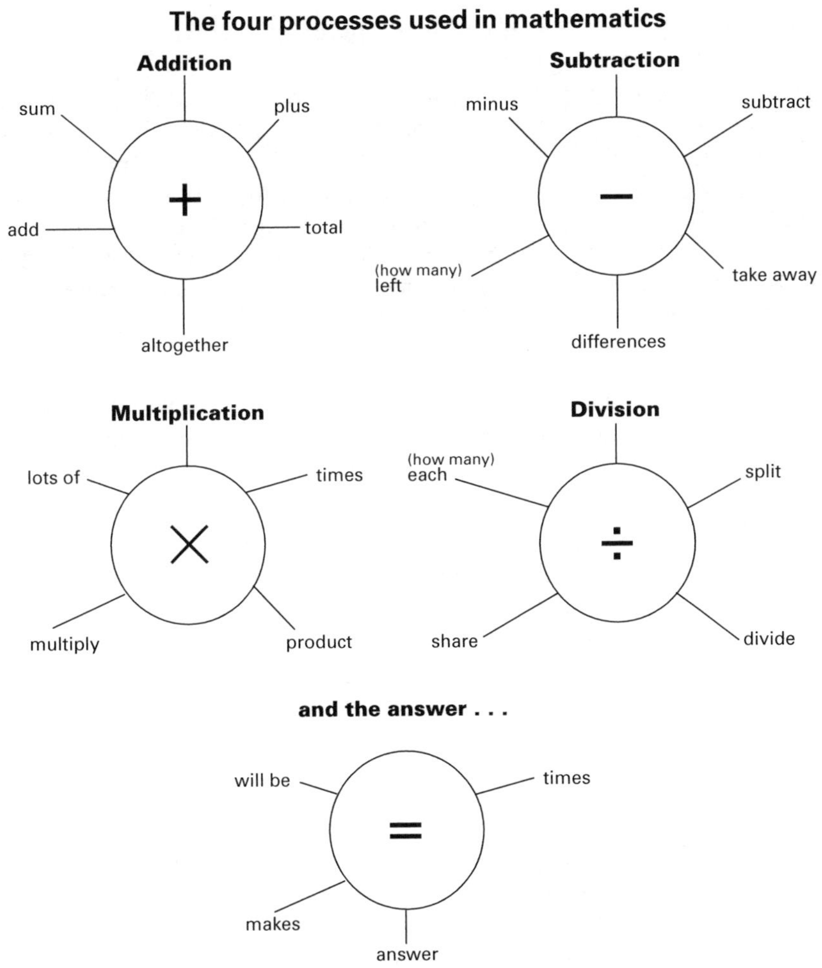

The four processes used in mathematics

Addition

sum
plus
add
+
total
altogether

Subtraction

minus
subtract
−
(how many) left
take away
differences

Multiplication

lots of
times
×
multiply
product

Division

(how many) each
split
÷
share
divide

and the answer . . .

will be
times
=
makes
answer

Figure 4.1 Henderson (1999) has produced some useful visual representations of the language which is used interchangeably to describe the four processes used in mathematics.

- Difficulty with long-term verbal memory.
  Tables: learning to the tune of pop songs or nursery rhymes can help some children.
  Visual cueing may always be needed for some children.
- Once a complex problem has been understood verbal reasoning skills are needed to review the alternative ways of reaching the goal and deciding which is the most efficient or appropriate strategy for that example. The identification of what is salient can be as important in maths as in literacy.

Some children with poor language are able to compensate by using strong visual/spatial reasoning skills – but don't expect them to be able to explain their reasoning.

- Children may have difficulty deciding what equipment they may need to support them with a mathematical task.
- Learning how to use equipment such as a number line or table square is best demonstrated rather than explained verbally.

> **Case Study: 'Naomi'**
>
> Naomi at age six years, had profound difficulties in retrieving language. However, she had a very strong visual memory which allowed her to associate symbols with the number of dots or blocks they represented. In this way she was able to carry out simple number operation without having to retrieve number names. By working in this way, aided by signing, Naomi gradually built a memory for number names in a meaningful and motivating way, drawing on her visual strengths.

Sequencing in Space and Time

Much of the early maths vocabulary and many early concepts involve both sequencing and time, e.g. first, next to, last. Children with language problems experience particular difficulties with these.

A poor sense of personal time such as estimating how long a task may take or anticipating the end of a lesson and, therefore, how much time is left to finish, may make task organisation a problem. Time is also relative so that five minutes finishing the maths task may feel very different from five minutes playing football. Without sophisticated language, it is hard to explain this type of experience.

Children may read digital time but have no idea about whether that means it is nearly playtime or after lunch. Learning to use a clock face may be a hard task. Time is an abstract concept and we often trying to represent it verbally, e.g. one minute as one unit of time, or the idea of half an hour when 'half' is not secure. This is a hard exercise in conceptual mapping, especially if visual support is not available. Visual timetables can help with both sequencing and the development of a sense of personal time. Any problem solving that assumes a knowledge of time concepts is likely to be difficult.

Mental maths

An ability to calculate mentally lies at the heart of numeracy. You should emphasise mental methods from the early years onwards, with regular opportunities for all pupils to develop the different skills involved.

(National Numeracy Strategy

Children with speech and language problems will find the vocabulary used in mental maths questions difficult to understand, and may well struggle with the demands being made on their auditory memory, ability to sequence and ability to identify salient information.

Children with speech and language difficulties are likely to experience problems with the following example of mental calculation:

> Mum sent John to the shop to buy lollipops for his birthday party. She gave him a £1 coin and told him to buy 6 lollipops costing 15p each. She told him he could keep the change. How much did he spend and how much money could he keep?

Potential difficulties are:

Verbal comprehension: the child may not understand the question.

Auditory memory: as the question is at the end of the problem, the child will have forgotten the important information that has preceded it.

Salience: the question is so long the child will not sift out those pieces of information essential to solving the problem. He/she may for example think that 'mum', the 'party' and the 'shop' are vital pieces of information for solving the problem.

Verbal reasoning: as the problem is presented in a linguistic form, language is needed to mediate in order to solve it. Also, without these skills the child could not use analogy to work out that 'money' and 'change' are the same thing in the context of this question.

Vocabulary: the child may not understand that money is the same thing as 'change' or that a coin is the word used to refer to units of money.

Sequencing: the sequence of the presentation may not match the sequence needed for the child to solve the problem.

The following strategies for *support* can be used.

- Teach the children the language involved in the problem as it may be known in one context and not in another, e.g. 'altogether' may be understood as 'something we do all together'.
- Use a flow chart to give visual support for the stages of the problem-solving process.
- Discuss and establish which parts of the question are salient and which are redundant.
- Simplify the remaining part of the question.
- Put the remaining part of the question in a sequence that the children will understand: order of mention equals order of action.
- Use real objects to assist memory at first and then replace with pictures as part of the sequence of developing the skill of remembering and working with abstract symbols.
- For recording purposes, show the children how to use colour coding or other visual markers, e.g. always put the total amount spent in a square or a triangle in order to scaffold the children's learning from a concrete to an abstract process.
- Use visual support to provide help with calculations. Use a number line and/or a number square. The number line must be vertical with the lowest number at the bottom, so that it corresponds to mathematical language such as 'high' or 'low' in numbers.
- Ask the child to give a simple explanation of how he/she solved the problem.

Motor planning and using equipment

A significant number of children with speech and language impairment also experience developmental coordination difficulties (DCD)/dyspraxia. This is usually most immediately apparent in their handwriting and how they attempt to set out their work.

The accurate recording of numbers is an integral part of getting the correct answer in maths because number reversals or column drift can lead to calculation errors. Setting out vertical addition or subtraction can be helped by using squared paper: the square size should reflect the size of the child's writing.

Children with dyspraxia associated with their speech and language impairment may have difficulties interpreting and producing maps, diagrams, graphs or charts.

Those children who have difficulties executing their motor plan (DCD) may have problems with using mathematical equipment, e.g. a ruler. This is a surprisingly complex skill which involves:

– knowing where to place the ruler on the paper
– knowing which end to start
– holding the ruler with sufficient pressure so that it does not slip on the paper, using the support hand
– using the preferred hand to make a mark on the paper without displacing the ruler.

A ruler is possibly the most simple form of mathematical equipment to use; a compass would for example present an even more complex motor-skill challenge.

Non-standard units of measurement are now frequently used in the classroom. Using such non-standard units, e.g. hand span for measuring distance, requires a high degree of motor skill which may present a motor challenge which takes precedence over the task goal.

In such cases, it is always helpful to find a way of achieving the goal for the task in a way which does not have a complex motor skill component.

These areas of difficulty and the strategies which may be used to support the children in their learning are discussed in more detail in *Inclusion for Children with Dyspraxia/DCD* (Ripley 2001).

Chapter 5

Sample subjects through the key stages

This chapter begins by considering the impact of receptive and expressive language difficulties upon speaking and listening, science, history and geography at Key Stages 1 and 2.

Introduction

Speaking and Listening: Key Stage 1

Difficulties which might be experienced by children with limited receptive language	**The impact of receptive and/or expressive language difficulties on the responses made by pupils**
1. Understanding stories at word/sentence/text level.	1. Poorly developed language skills can inhibit story telling, accounts of personal experience, etc.
2. Lack of awareness of the range of appropriate styles of verbal and non-verbal interaction.	2. Expressive language difficulties minimise opportunities for verbal interaction.
3. Difficulties with listening and attention and poor memory skills.	3. Poor memory skills impact on all areas of expressive language.
4. Poor social interaction skills, e.g. judgement of social situations, turn-taking, awareness of listener's needs.	4. Poor use of language in social situations, e.g. choice of language, style of language and how to start/finish a conversation.
5. Poor understanding of grammatical forms and how these can change meaning.	5. Poor expressive language limits the expression of meaning.
6. Poor understanding of question forms, e.g. when, what, who, why, how, which.	6. Asking for information is difficult without being able to use question forms.
7. Poor understanding of the rules of putting sounds together in words has an effect upon how words are restored in one's 'internal dictionary'.	7. Poor pronunciation interferes with communication and impacts on literacy acquisition.

Difficulties which might be experienced by children with limited receptive language	**The impact of receptive and/or expressive language difficulties on the responses made by pupils**

Speaking and Listening at Key Stage 2 and beyond

1. Difficulties with understanding abstract ideas.

   1. Poorly developed language skills can inhibit story telling, accounts of events and procedures.

2. Poor ability to predict.

   2. Poor ability to predict can inhibit the development of constructing a range of responses.

3. Poor social judgement skills inhibit the development of insight and the teacher's use of non-literal language may not be understood.

   3. Spoken language remains at a literal level and this makes a major impact upon narrative and poetry.

4. Poor general understanding produces difficulties with salience.

   4. Lack of understanding of salience produces irrelevant and inappropriate responses and changes of topic.

5. Poor understanding of aspects of language, e.g. metaphor, inference, idioms.

   5. Production of tangential inappropriate and irrelevant responses.

6. Lack of understanding of complex meanings, particularly the decontextualised language of the classroom.

   6. Lack of understanding affects insight which compromises the ability to evaluate, understand role, share ideas and opinions and empathise.

7. Poorly developed memory skills reduce the retention of verbal material.

   7. Phonological skills impact on all areas of spoken language and literacy acquisition.

8. Lack of awareness of listener's needs.

   8. Poorly developed skills of clarification, initiation and termination of topics of conversation result in the breakdown of these conversations.

9. Poor understanding of question forms.

   9. Poor ability to ask questions for (a) getting help and (b) eliciting information.
      Some children may not realise that they have failed to understand and need to ask a question.

Science Key Stage 1	**Difficulties which might be experienced by children with limited receptive language**	**The impact of receptive and/or expressive language difficulties on the responses made by pupils**
	1. Failure to understand question forms.	1. Inappropriate responses and an inability to use question forms.
	2. Lack of understanding of the language of science. Finding it confusing that words can have a scientific meaning as well as an everyday meaning.	2. Poor ability to respond appropriately to instructions for specific tasks. This may be a memory problem and/or a difficulty with the complexity of the language that is used.
	3. Poor generalisation of knowledge.	3. Inability to predict and to use language to mediate in problem solving.
	4. Lack of understanding of language associated with first-hand experience, e.g. specific vocabulary for the topic.	4. Word-finding difficulties may disrupt verbal expression.
	5. Failure to understand and appreciate analogy.	5. Failure to recognise hazards and risks when working with living things and materials.
	6. Lack of understanding of the language of cause and effect.	6. Poor sequencing makes it hard to follow through an experience in a prescribed order.

Science Key Stage 2 and beyond	**Difficulties which might be experienced by children with limited receptive language**	**The impact of receptive and/or expressive language difficulties on the responses made by pupils**
	1. Difficulties with understanding cause/effect and salience.	1. Impacts on verbal reasoning and difficulties with formulating questions.
	2. Difficulties with understanding inference with both first hand experience and the use of secondary sources.	2. Impacts on verbal reasoning and appropriateness of response.
	3. Difficulties with generalising knowledge and understanding analogy.	3. Inability to mobilise general knowledge and their ability to apply it to a specific problem.
	4. Poor conceptual understanding.	4. Impacts on the application of science to relevant areas, e.g. personal health.
	5. Poor understanding of vocabulary.	5. Limits ability to describe and explain, e.g. the behaviour of living things, materials and processes.

*History
Key Stage 1*

Difficulties which might be experienced by children with limited receptive language	The impact of receptive and/or expressive language difficulties on the responses made by pupils
1. Failure to understand even the most basic language, e.g. that objects have labels, inhibits the building of an understanding of the world.	1. Impacts on links between objects and events on salience, cause and effect, on inference, generalisation of knowledge.
2. May learn in a rote fashion, e.g. stories about the lives of people.	2. Unable to draw any useful conclusions or appreciate the relevance of information. Responses will therefore be superficial.
3. Difficulties with time concepts and placing themselves within a time frame even within the present, the understanding of sequences and relevant vocabulary, e.g. before/after.	3. Difficulties with using the common time frames of history teaching, e.g. 'yesterday', 'when my grandma was very young'.
4. Poor understanding of cause and effect.	4. Inhibits explanations of why people did things and the outcome of that action.

*History
Key Stage 2
and beyond*

Difficulties which might be experienced by children with limited receptive language	The impact of receptive and/or expressive language difficulties on the responses made by pupils
1. Difficulties with time concepts and an internal sense of the passing of time.	1. Impacts on the ability to place people and events within a chronological framework.
2. Failure to understand different kinds of vocabulary (concepts, labels, etc.) inhibits the building of a knowledge of the world.	2. Impacts on the development and expression of ideas, beliefs and attitudes.
3. Poor understanding of cause and effect.	3. Inhibits the ability to formulate and express descriptions and the identification of reasons for and results of historical events, situations and changes.
4. Difficulties with salience and generalisation. Also with using language to mediate in the process of verbal reasoning.	4. Impacts on description and the formulation of links between main events, situations and changes.
5. Difficulties with verbal memory.	5. Inhibits recalling, selecting and organising historical information.

Geography Key Stage 1	**Difficulties which might be experienced by children with limited receptive language**	**The impact of receptive and/or expressive language difficulties on the responses made by pupils**
	1. Difficulties with understanding question forms, particularly question words.	1. Difficulties with framing appropriate questions to elicit relevant information, e.g. where/what?
	2. Difficulties with understanding different kinds of vocabulary inhibits the building knowledge of the world.	2. Inhibits the awareness of the world beyond their own locality. • Inhibits appropriate use of the spatial vocabulary linked with the exploration of surroundings. • Produces difficulties in formulating judgements in order to compare and contrast and express views.
	3. Difficulties with verbal memory.	3. Difficulties with following directions, e.g. 'in front', 'near', 'far', 'north'.
	4. Difficulties with understanding cause and effect.	4. Difficulties with generating hypothesis, e.g. about the effects of weather on people and surroundings.

Geography Key Stage 2 and beyond	**Difficulties which might be experienced by children with limited receptive language**	**The impact of receptive and/or expressive language difficulties on the responses made by pupils**
	1. Difficulties in understanding question forms, particularly question words.	1. Difficulties with framing appropriate questions to elicit relevant information, e.g. 'does it?', 'can it?'
	2. Difficulties with understanding different kinds of vocabulary.	2. Impacts on the ability to analyse evidence, draw conclusions and communicate ideas. Also to compare and contrast localities.
	3. Difficulties in understanding links between words, ideas, events.	3. Inhibits the awareness of the world beyond their own locality.
	4. Difficulties understanding inference and salience and making generalisations.	4. Impacts on the awareness of the characteristics of localities, similarities/differences, change and the broader context.

The more obvious signs of a speech and language disorder tend to recede as children progress through the education system. However, some or all of the following characteristics may be identifiable among secondary aged students with speech and language impairment.

- Spoken language difficulties, which may be evident in both comprehension and expressive language, including difficulties with syntax and morphology, vocabulary acquisition and/or retrieval. These may be in evidence in the educational setting although the students may appear to 'get by' in social contexts. Some may struggle even in social contexts such as the girl described in the Case Study at the end of Chapter 1.
- The students may have noticeable difficulties with the more subtle aspects of pragmatic function and with any task or interaction which involves inference and implication, in particular those which involve the use of figurative language (idioms, metaphors, puns, jokes).
- The capacity to understand words and concepts where the meaning is context-determined and relative, and perhaps more importantly to use the context to help identify the meaning, can also be an area of difficulty. For example, the Year 9 boy who when told someone's pregnant sister was in labour thought that she had joined a political party.
- Difficulties at the level of abstract reasoning, integrating and generalising what they know into broad, abstract concepts and memorising unrelated topics.
- The difficulties with spoken language will be reflected in text comprehension and written language production.
- Some students who have a history of phonological problems may experience ongoing difficulties with spelling and the decoding component of reading.

Within this general profile each student will have their own individual profile of strengths and needs. For many students with speech and language impairment, the difficulties which they have experienced at primary school will persist into the secondary phrase of their education. This may be particularly noticeable in key areas such as:

- listening and sustaining auditory attention;
- remembering what is said to them and the need for visual support for this skill;
- learning new vocabulary and using familiar vocabulary in a new context;
- understanding non-literal language whether spoken or written;
- understanding complex sentences whether spoken or written;
- word-finding problems;
- understanding key concepts of cause and effect, time and what is important or salient in a particular context.

Embarrassing experiences encountered by students in the past may have made them reluctant to respond to questions or join in with discussions when part of the class group. Enduring difficulties with the organisation of their expressive language may compound this understandable reluctance to participate. Rehearsal with the classroom assistant of the form and content of

Language and communication difficulties in Key Stages 3–4

possible answers, prior to a whole-class session can encourage more active participation. A few students may still have difficulty with understanding and formulating questions. This skill will need practice and this is most effectively done in the context of the curriculum.

Many children will have an understanding and an ability to use the basic grammatical structures of the English language before the transfer to secondary school. However, when these structures are combined into complex sentences with subordinate clauses they may still be hard to understand. It is, therefore, important for subject teachers to be aware not only of any new topic vocabulary that they introduce, but also of the complexity of their instructions and explanations at a grammatical level. It is good practice for all teachers sometimes to tape record themselves and analyse the tape.

There are few classroom opportunities to work directly on grammar either at primary or secondary school except by modelling the correct grammatical structure, e.g.

> *'Thems three, Miss.'*
> *'Yes, that's right ____, there are three.'*

Direct work on grammar and vocabulary at secondary school is often most appropriately addressed using a written text. Activities can then be planned for the students to use the new structures and vocabulary in their own spoken and written language.

Students who experience receptive language problems may not always be aware that they have not understood an explanation or an instruction. It may only become apparent when they have done the wrong thing and possibly been in trouble as a consequence. By the same token, they may not be aware when they need to ask for help. The section on comprehension monitoring for spoken and written language gives more details about these areas of difficulty (p. 38).

Basic Interpersonal Communication Skills to Cognitive Academic Language Processing (BICS ➔ CALP)

Early language skills are acquired in the context of real-life interactions with people. These basic interpersonal communication skills (BICS) are well established for most children when they enter school. From the time children enter the education system they are increasingly exposed to more abstract decontextualised language. Cognitive academic language processing (CALP) takes five to seven years to develop in 'average' learners and it becomes significantly more crucial in accessing the curriculum when children transfer to secondary school.

In every Year 7 there will be a significant number of children including those with speech and language impairment, who find it hard to understand and to use abstract decontextualised language. There will be others whose preferred learning style is for visual and simultaneous processing rather than auditory and sequential processing. All students who are struggling with 'CALP' language will benefit from having the traditional 'chalk and talk' reinforced by experiential learning, demonstration, modelling, visual cueing and visual presentations.

The ability to carry out cognitive academic language processing can be supported if there are strategies in place to help the children understand the more abstract, decontextualised language which is being introduced. The model proposed by Cummins (1986) provide an essential framework for this process (see Figures 5.1 and 5.2). Cummins maintains that if the transition from Quadrant 1 to Quadrant 4 takes place by an indirect route rather than an abrupt transition, children with restricted CALP can develop the skills which are needed to access the secondary curriculum.

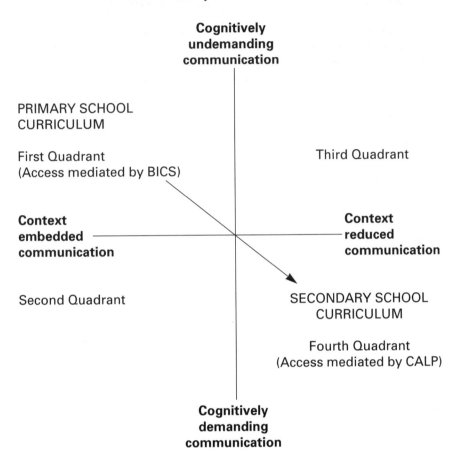

Figure 5.1 Principal language orientation of the curriculum

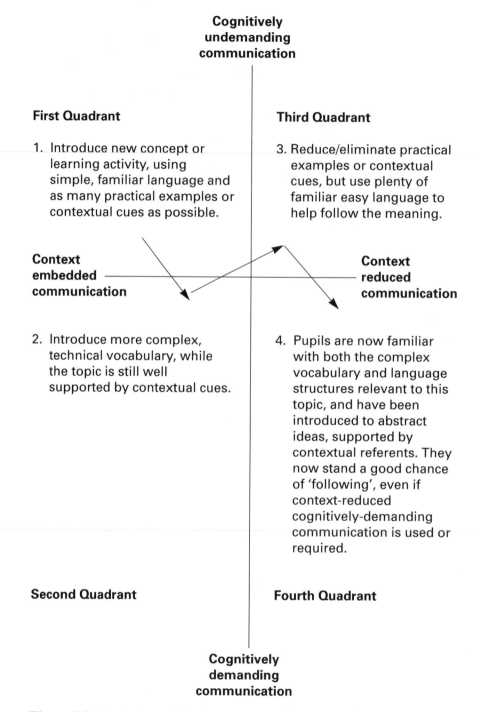

Figure 5.2 Curriculum delivery: a sequence for successful learning

Chapter 6

Strategies to support learning

Attention control, like motor skills and language, follows a developmental sequence. Small babies are attracted to any novel stimulus such as a new sound or pretty lights, but as they develop they are able to hold their attention on tap for activities which attract them for increasingly long periods of time. Sometimes it is difficult to shift anyone's attention if they are really engrossed. Think of a ten-year-old deep into the latest Harry Potter book. As children develop, they gain more control over the focus of their attention and will learn to give attention to what adults ask them to do, rather than only following their own interests. This voluntary control of attention begins to develop from the age of three to four years. Adults may choose to focus their attention on many types of stimulus – visual, tactile, taste, smell – as well as sound. Taken out to a wonderful restaurant, we may choose to focus our attention and sustain it on taste and fail to listen to what our fellow guests are saying. Too long and we may seem very rude!

Attention and listening

The stages in the development of attention were described by Reynell in 1976 (see Chapter 1). For some children the development of their attention control is relatively slow. This may be because they have a general developmental delay and so the attention control is in line with their other areas of development. Other children may be reaching their developmental milestones in most areas, but show a more specific delay in the development of attention control which may appear to be 'stuck' at an early stage. These children may be identified as having Attention Deficit Disorder (ADD).

Children who have delayed language development may be described by their teachers as having poor attention because they are restless at story time or during other carpet-time activities. In these cases, it is important to distinguish between children who have difficulty focusing attention on auditory input, i.e. listening, from children who have fleeting attention in any modality. Some children who have been described as having poor attention control based on their ability to focus and sustain attention on auditory stimuli, i.e. listening, may well be able to focus their attention on visual and visual-motor activities that do not involve listening. Careful observation of children when they are engaged in a range of activities should help to distinguish children who find listening hard from those who have a general difficulty with attention control. Children with language problems frequently have problems listening (Figure 6.1).

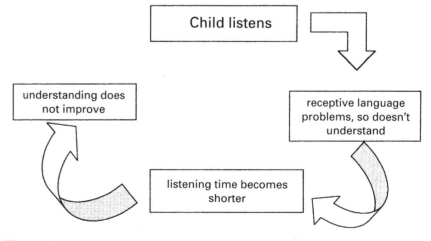

Figure 6.1

The first step in improving listening skills is to check that the child understands what is being said. There have been many excellent books entirely devoted to the subject of promoting listening skills, which include:

Activities for Speaking and Listening Part 1 Ages 3–7, Part 2 Ages 7–11, AFASIC Publications with the Speech and Language Therapy Department Hounslow and Spelthorne Health Authority
Early Listening Skills by Diana Williams, Winslow Press
Listening Skills, Key Stage 1 Levels 1 and 2, Rickerby and Lambert The Questions Publishing Co.

As a general rule it is more productive to follow through the normal developmental sequence to improve listening skills. It is essential that the activities are compatible with the child's particular level of listening, for example, they must be able to detect a sound before they can learn to recognise it. A useful sequence to follow is that suggested by Diana Williams in *Early Listening Skills*:

- discovering sound
- exploring sound makers
- sound or silence
- simple discrimination
- sound recognition
- finding sound
- fine discrimination.

The skills of rhythm and sequencing, and listening to spoken commands, are more advanced abilities which also rely on auditory memory skills.

'Six of the best' for younger children

- Tapes of environmental sounds, animal noises, instrument sounds, to recognise, or use real objects with teacher and pupil taking turns to make sounds behind a screen.
- Put objects on a table, child picks up objects as they are mentioned in the story.
- Clapping, putting a counter in a pot when children hear a particular phrase or word.
- Spotting the 'wrong' word in a story, e.g. Goldilocks and the three 'tears'.
- Keys of the Kingdom: Keys are passed round a circle of children. One child is blindfolded in the middle. If this child hears the keys, they point to where they are. If correct, it is the other child's turn to be blindfolded.
- Toy telephone: Each child is told a telephone number (the number of digits can be varied) which they can use to call a friend on the toy telephone. If the child makes a mistake, the operator/teacher says 'wrong number'. A delay can be introduced by telling all the children in the group their friend's number at the start of the game.

'Six of the best' for older children

If older children are not listening well, it could be because they find it hard to switch from *monitoring* attention to *focused* attention. Whatever we are doing, washing up, writing an essay or chatting to friends, we are monitoring the auditory environment for anything which might be significant such as the mention of our name. In the past, this screening process, of which we are largely unaware, would have been useful to alert us to sounds of danger so that we could bring our focused attention into action as a prelude to flight or fight. Some people are not good at switching from monitoring attention to focused attention, for example when the teacher starts talking, unless they are supported to make the switch e.g. by someone calling their name or telling them to stop what they are doing and waiting for eye contact as a signal that attention is focused on listening.

- Before starting a verbal explanation in class give children a written list of short questions, with picture support for some children. Go through the list and explain that they should be listening for the answers. This helps to focus listening attention.
- Ensure a quiet environment with as few auditory distractions as possible. Seat the child experiencing difficulty near the front of the class so that they are not distracted by children in front.
- Limit the time that focused auditory attention is required and give well marked 'breaks' in the form of activities or question and answer sessions.
- Ensure that the child is comfortably seated at a table and on a chair of the right height.
- Support verbal instructions with written instructions or present in a pictorial form.
- Teacher's verbal presentation is accompanied by natural gesture in order to maintain interest and attention.

Remembering

It is possible that the child has immature listening skills rather than a memory problem *per se* and so the teaching of active listening skills may be a first step. These are described in the previous section 'Attention and listening'.

Although memory may appear to improve if we practice remembering, this is usually because we have developed more effective strategies to help us to remember.

Principles

- We all remember things better if they are of interest and relevance to us, so link new information to the familiar and areas of interest to the child.
- Things which are, or can be, put to practical use tend to be remembered better.
- Skills and knowledge which we practise or we use regularly are those retained best.

Teaching strategies to support auditory memory difficulties

- Experiential learning: doing, watching, participating in the activity should be used to back up any verbal instructions.
- Visual cueing for equipment:
  - Teacher/LSA prepares a pack of cue card pictures showing the items of equipment which are regularly used in the class. The 'you will need' instruction is backed up by dealing the relevant cards onto a velcro strip on a child's table or better still, larger picture cards can be used as a whole-class prompt. All will benefit. One child will not be singled out.

– For activities for which regular items of equipment are needed a 'Have I got?' visual checklist can be used. More discrete written or symbol checklists can be used for older students.

– Self-cueing using pictures/icons as the teacher is talking.

Examples of visual notes using icons

'First, will you do the two times table worksheet? When you've finished that, go and get your snack out of your lunch box. Then go and wash your hands.' (Figure 6.2.)

What weren't they told? – 'Take the key and unlock the grey cupboard. Get the musical instruments out of the cupboard and lock the cupboard up. On your way back to the classroom go into the office and pick up the register. While you're in the office, ask Mrs Gutherless to ring your mum and tell her that you're feeling better. Take the musical instruments back to the classroom. By then it'll be home time, so you can put your chair on the table.' (Figure 6.3.)

Are there any instructions which are too complicated? – 'If you're working in the wet area, the blue group, you've to be sensible. You've to be careful with the glue and the scissors. Don't stick one big piece of material for the whole shape of the bird: cut the material into small pieces and put different material to make up a pattern for the body of the bird, that way it looks much better when it's finished.' (*Spotlight on Special Educational Needs* Daines *et al.* 1996) (Figure 6.4.)

- Visual cueing for process
  Blank flow charts with two to six 'boxes' can be photocopied and filled in by the child or an LSA as needed.
  Children working with an adult in a group to decide what has to be done and in what order is a helpful learning exercise.
  - Using mnemonics: for example, **A**ll **E**lephants **I**n **O**ld **U**nderpants, for the vowel sounds.

Exercises to practise remembering (Key Stages 1 and 2)

Try to make memory training fun by incorporating it into class and group activities. The activities should start off by being quite simple and then gradually be increased in complexity. There are several ways of making activities more demanding. Ways of making the task *harder* are:

– increase the number of items to choose between
– increasing the number of items to recall
– increase the perceptual or conceptual similarity of the items used
– requiring that the child remembers items in the right order
– introducing a delay before the child responds
– introducing a distracting task before allowing the child to respond
– increasing the complexity of any verbal instructions
– putting a time-limit on the activity.

Figure 6.2

Figure 6.3

Figure 6.4

Memory Games fall into six main categories and some examples are given below to illustrate the type of activities involved.

Action games

- 'Simon Says,' with the instructions becoming more complex over time e.g. *'touch you left ear with the thumb of your right hand'*.
- 'Find me' games – children are asked to fetch item(s) located around the classroom.
- 'Listen and Do' games – children have a set of toys and are asked to do things with them, e.g. 'The Farm': *'Put the farmer and the cow in the barn.'*
- Dressing up games – children remember what they have been told to put on.

Listing games

- Grandmother's Trunk: Child 1 – a blue dress; Child 2 – a blue dress and a shoe; etc.
- I went shopping and I bought . . .

Message games

- Whispering a message round the group.
- Deliver a simple message to a pre-prepared adult and increase message complexity gradually.
- A message with a time gap of increasing length before it can be delivered.
- A password which has to be remembered to get access to favourite activities, e.g. the computer.

Listen and repeat

- Rhymes and nursery rhymes.
- Phrases and sentences – if they can be made funny.
- Telephone numbers in the context of role play games.

What is missing?

- Read out a list of items, repeat with one item missing.
- The same can be done with names, digits, rhymes, stories.

Active remembering for older students (Key Stages 2–4)

- Read or listen – write down what you remember
  – check and add what is forgotten
  – rewrite.
- Read or listen – make a mind map or concept map
  – put what you need to remember in a diagram.
- Key word a text by underlining or using a highlighter pen. Represent the key concepts on a diagram.
- Keep practising the recall of any information you need to remember
  – use imagining like the Ancient Greeks
  – use the tunes of pop songs
  – make a rap.
- Learning new vocabulary – some words have multiple meanings and a semantic web may help to clarify these: if you come across a new word:

- look it up in the dictionary
- think of a visual cue or association which will help you remember, e.g. thermometer – the mum hit her
- use it in your speech, making a point of bringing the new word into a conversation at least once a day for the first week.

Vocabulary learning strategies

Vocabulary learning is a process which is ongoing and covers every area of a child's life, at home and in school. As the child progresses through the key stages the amount and complexity of vocabulary increases rather than decreases. This poses particular difficulties for children whose vocabulary is already delayed or disordered.

Children need to learn vocabulary before they use it. Comprehension refers to the child's ability to learn and retain new words which can be, for example nouns (chair, cat), verbs (run, throw), adverbs (quickly, suddenly), plus all other classes of words.

When a child learns a new word it is 'filed away' in two different ways. Firstly, he/she has to process the sound structure of the word, e.g. what sounds make up the word, how many syllables it contains. Next the word has to be processed in terms of meaning, e.g. what group or category of word does it belong to, its function, what it looks like, feels like and so on. This way of filing the word away can be thought of as a mental dictionary but instead of being organised alphabetically the words are grouped in terms of meaning so that words closely associated in meaning will be closely connected.

Once a child's word learning (receptive vocabulary) is delayed and/or disordered, their ability to use vocabulary will also be delayed and/or disordered. Their expressive language will lack detail and will contain many non-specific or sometimes inaccurate words. (A child with poor expressive vocabulary may not necessarily have word retrieval difficulties.)

- Be realistic about the amount of vocabulary the child can be expected to learn. If given too much they will 'switch off' and is likely to learn very little or nothing at all. Choose a core vocabulary for a topic or subject area. It can then be checked at the end of the topic/term in order to monitor progress.
- By using classroom based activities, planned opportunities can be arranged for the child to generalise and consolidate the new vocabulary. Vocabulary needs to be revisited and 'over learned'.

Teaching new vocabulary

New vocabulary is best taught using a hierarchical approach (Rinaldi 1998) so that the core vocabulary chosen will include topic/subject and category labels and be taught in a systematic way using the curriculum. The sequence suggested is as follows:

- Ensure that the vocabulary and concept teaching is topic based – that is, teach related words which can be group into sets, categories and groups, e.g. living things can be divided into animals and plants (see Figure 6.5).

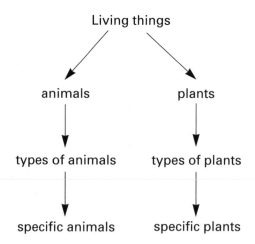

Figure 6.5

Teach category labels, e.g. living things, animals, mini beasts and the vocabulary and concepts within these.

- Always begin with the big picture, e.g. habitats, myself. Regularly refer back to this at the start of each lesson.
- Brainstorm the topic in a hierarchical way (as above).
- Explain why the child is learning the vocabulary, e.g. link to real life – food categories can be linked to shopping.
- Use vocabulary/concepts that are already known to the child in order to learn new vocabulary, e.g. when introducing 'habitats' start by talking about where the child or a pet lives.
- Place in a context – link the vocabulary to real-life situations whenever possible and use real objects, go to real places.
- Use multi-sensory reinforcement:
    - visual (real objects, colour, pictures, gestures signs)
    - tactile (feeling shape, materials, a sequence of movements).
- Say as well as listen – at each stage encourage the child to say (describe words by meaning), e.g. each time put an item into its group category 'an apple is a fruit and it's food, you get it at the shop'. Also describe by
    - attribute (shape, size, colour)
    - association (it goes in the fridge with the other food).
- Make sure words are learned correctly with reference to their sound structure, i.e. by syllable structure: e – le – phant.
    - first sound in the word
    - rhyming – what rhymes with cat?
    - rehearsal – saying the words aloud.
- More subtle and complex aspects of the vocabulary should not be introduced until the key groups have been learned, e.g. exceptions, ambiguity.
- Provide opportunities for lots of reinforcement and repetition of key words, i.e. revisit the vocabulary even when the topic is finished and reinforce the vocabulary concepts in as many different contexts as possible.

Vocabulary extension

Each of the levels can be expanded and reinforced by using any of the following (depending on the age of the child).

Topic: Living Things

Nouns	*Verbs*	*Adjectives*
plant/animal names	ways of eating, moving, etc.	describe animals
cat	purr	furry
whale	swim	slimy
seagull	fly	feathery

Topic: Habitats

Show how one animal can belong to more than one category:

	Land	**Sea/lakes**	**Sky**
Hot countries	Turtle	Turtle	
	Snake	Flamingo	Flamingo
Cold countries	Penguin	Penguin	
	Arctic Fox	Snow Goose	Snow Goose

Word Trees

These show the hierarchical nature of groups:

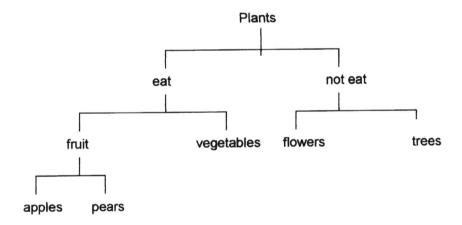

Figure 6.6

Word Wheels

These can be done in several ways:

- Provide the key word at the centre of the wheel and then the child thinks of associated words (including nouns, adjectives, verbs, etc.) and thinks why they go with the key word.
- Provide all the associated words, the child names the key word.
- Provide the key word associated and non-associated word. The child has to decide which go with the keywords and why.

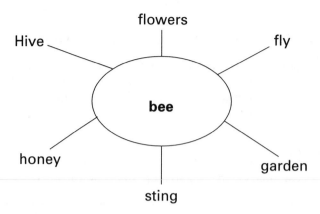

Figure 6.8

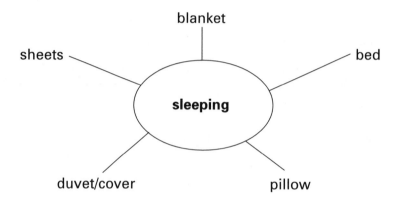

Figure 6.8

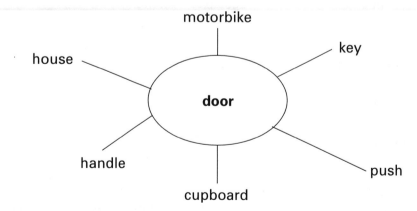

Figure 6.9

Word maps

These can be used to connect ideas and expand single words into sentences, e.g. people eat plants.

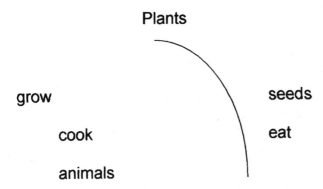

Figure 6.10

Mind maps are also relevant, see 'Pre-preparation of text and key wording' later in this Chapter.

Useful topic lists are contained in both *Living Language* (Locke 1985) and *Language Concepts to Access Learning* (Rinaldi 1998).

For successful retrieval, children with speech and language impairment should be taught vocabulary in a systematic, hierarchical and repetitive way (see previous section of this chapter). To further aid recall of a word it is possible to offer cues to support:

Strategies to support word-finding problems Key Stages 1–4

- accessing the word by the appropriate meaning (semantic);
- accessing the grammatical information (is it a noun, verb, etc., how does it fit into a sentence);
- accessing the phonological information (that is the sound structure of the word).

Children can be taught strategies to aid word retrieval and research has shown that they benefit most from an approach combining the above (bullet points) plus the use of natural gesture for signing.

For each key word taught, children should learn all the features about it:-

- Semantic
  - what category it belongs to
  - what other categories could it go in
  - what it's made of
  - what you do with it
  - what does it go with, e.g. cup and saucer
  - where would you see it
  - who would use it/make it, etc.
  - what does it smell like
  - what does it feel like.
- Grammatical
  - what group of words does it fit into, i.e. the name of something (noun), an action (verb), a descriptive word (adjective)
  - where does it fit in a sentence.

(Grammatical knowledge is more useful for older children who will have been taught how words have different functions in a sentence and can be classified in this way.)

- Phonological (also referred to as 'phonemic')
  - what sound it starts with
  - what sound it ends with
  - what does it rhyme with/sound like
  - how many syllables it has.

The children can sort further words (key vocabulary) according to one of the above features (semantic, grammatical, phonological). They can then recall as many words as they can from one set. All words can be accompanied by natural gesture or a sign if it has been taught. It is a very useful strategy and one we all use from time to time!

- The children could make a 'category dictionary' for new topic vocabulary or any other new vocabulary which needs to be learned. The dictionary contains category pages (categories are selected by the children) so that when a new word is to be learned, the appropriate category is selected and the word written on that page. The category can then be divided into smaller groups of words and within the smaller group the target word should be written and the first sound underlined or coloured. Any other information can be added which might help recall, e.g. 'what do you do with it?'

The dictionary can be used flexibly: by the children when they have forgotten a key word or a new word – they look up the appropriate category page; or by an adult who gives clues (a type of guessing game) so the children can find the target word.

- Encourage the children to remember the 'tip of the tongue' cues. These are to help yourself and others:
  - think of the first sound in the word
  - try to think where it fits in a sentence 'mum played tennis with a _____ and ball'
  - picture what the word looks like in your head
  - gesture or sign it
  - think of another word that means nearly the same (a kind of bat)
  - say what it's used for (to hit a ball).
- Using key vocabulary play guessing games which can, at first, be led by an adult who gives the clues. Subsequently the children should be encouraged to give the clues.

Older children can be encouraged to participate in slightly harder activities, e.g. general pairs of opposites such as light/dark; play word-association games; give word definitions using categories, functions, word structure, etc.

Word-finding problems and reading in the early years (Key Stages 1–2)

Children who experience word-finding difficulties when talking may also have difficulty making the link between a written word and its meaning when they are reading. This may be frustrating for older students but significantly interfere with the acquisition of a sight vocabulary of high frequency words in young children. The work carried out by Daines and Ripley (1992) in a mainstream primary school showed that the use of signing was helpful in making the links between a written word and its meaning. The signing support was particularly useful for the abstract function words, e.g. 'from', 'when', which have a low network of meaning and are hard for many children to remember. Children will use signs to self-cue in reading as well as speaking if they have word-finding problems. In the study, signing was used alongside the usual methods of teaching reading in one of two parallel infant classes. The results indicated that:

- all children may benefit from signing during the initial stages of acquiring a sight vocabulary of high frequency words;
- signing is most effective with the 'function' words which have a low network of meaning (unlike 'mummy' or 'car');
- the children who had the lowest baseline scores for word recognition before the start of the intervention were most helped by the signing programme.

Signing may, therefore, be used to good effect as an additional element in a multi-sensory approach to reading in a mainstream school when children are acquiring a sight vocabulary. The use of finger spelling is a well-established technique to support children who have SLI with the discrimination of speech sounds and can be used to support the links between spoken sounds and written letters.

Teaching question forms

The first question form that children learn and use is by making their voices go up at the end of a phrase (inflection), e.g.:

'Mummy come?' – meaning 'are you coming now mummy', 'will you come with me mummy', etc.

The next form of questioning is by the use of question words:

'What' – refers to things
'Who' – refers to a person or persons
'Whom' – refers to a person or persons used as the object of a verb
'When' – refers to time
'Where' – refers to place
'How' – refers to procedure or method
'Whose' – refers to possession
'Which' – refers to selecting one of a known group
'How many/how much' – refers to number or amount
'Why' – refers to reason

As more question words are acquired, questions by inversion begin to appear, e.g. 'Can I . . .' After this, increasingly complex question forms begin to emerge which rely on more sophisticated grammar. Examples of these are as follows.

Tag questions. Tag questions are questions formed by adding a question phrase at the end of a sentence. Examples are 'I'm finished, <u>aren't I?</u>', 'She's not finished, <u>is she?</u>'.

Question forms using: progressive present, past and future tense verbs.

Present progressive – indicates that an action or event begun in the past is in progress at present and will likely continue into the future. Examples are 'Are you walking?', 'Are they walking?'.

Past progressive – indicates that an action or event began in the past and was in progress at a specific moment in the past. Examples are – 'Were we walking?', 'Was he walking?'.

Future progressive – indicates that an action or event will be in progress at a particular time in the future. Examples are 'Will I be walking?', 'Am I going to be walking?', 'Will we be walking?', 'Are we going to be walking?'.

Question forms using perfect, present, past and future tense verbs.

Present perfect – indicates that something happened before now at an indefinite time in the past. Examples are 'Have you finished?', 'Have they washed?'.

Past perfect – indicates that an action or event was completed before another action or event occurred or before another time in the past. Examples are 'Had you finished?', 'Had they finished?'.

Future perfect – indicates that an activity will be completed before another time or event in the future. Examples are 'Will you have been driving?', 'Will they have been drinking?'.

Question forms using perfect, progressive, present, past and future tense verbs.

Present, perfect, progressive – indicates the duration of an activity or event that began in the past and continues into the present. Examples are 'Has he been crying?', 'Have they been shouting?'.

Past, perfect, progressive – indicates the length of time of an activity or event that was in progress prior to another activity or time in the past. Examples are 'Will you have been fishing by then?', 'Will they have been fishing by then?'

Question forms using modal auxiliary verbs.

Modal auxiliary verbs accompany main verbs in sentences. They enable the speaker to express attitudes and feelings.

Probability or necessity – examples are 'Should bikers wear helmets?', 'Am I supposed to pay my coffee money on Friday?'.

Permission – examples are 'Could you pass the pepper, please?', 'May I sit here?'.

Question forms using the passive voice.

The **passive** form of verbs helps express the idea that someone or something is the object of an action. Examples are 'Was the child being protected by the dog?', 'Could the driver be prosecuted?'.

Negative Questions – examples are 'Doesn't he have a ticket?', 'Aren't you ready yet?'.

The examples quoted above are taken from Marilyn M. Toomey's book *Teaching Kids of All Ages to Ask Questions*. They demonstrate the extreme complexity of some question forms and the sophisticated knowledge and use of grammar needed by a child to be able to understand and use them. Those question forms relying on simpler grammatical constructions are most easily taught in context. There are many opportunities within the day to learn and practise these. For example, at registration time:

'Who is getting the register?'
'What is Jill doing?'
'Why are you late?'
'Where is George?'
'How are you?'
'When is assembly?'
'Will you please sit down.'

There are other opportunities to teach more complex grammatical forms, for example, teachers frequently ask children 'Have you been talking?' or 'What have you done with your ruler?'.

Structured activities are required to teach the more sophisticated and complex question forms to secondary aged children. For example, role play is a good vehicle for teaching question forms such as 'Would he have been happy doing that?', 'Was he supposed to have told his mother that?'.

The use of text also provides opportunities for working with these kinds of questions.

Whole-word approaches to reading and writing Key Stages 1 and 2

- An audiogram of a person speaking does not show any boundaries which correspond to separate words. Children learn the range of units of sound which correspond to a 'word' and we are reminded of this when we listen to an unfamiliar language and cannot work out where one word ends and another begins.

  It is a range because the actual sound pattern of a word will be different depending on the preceding and succeeding words.

  For some children who have difficulties with establishing these word boundaries when they listen to speech, it may help to have a picture or a written representation of the target word(s) to support their sound system and help them to discriminate.

  Learning words using picture or written representations on cards can help these children.
- Some children have great difficulty with the grammar of the language. They may have problems with the ordering of words in a sentence. A visual representation of word order using pictures or symbols, or words depending on the age of the child may help with learning word order and can act as their written output.

75

In the classroom there are few opportunities to work specifically on grammar unless this is linked to some form of 'written' output (Daines *et al.* 1996).

Asking LSAs who scribe for a child to write down the child's output verbatim gives a useful record of what grammatical structures need to be taught. It also enables progress in grammatical development to be monitored and ensures that what is taught is being generalised into spontaneous expressive language.

> LSA sentence: The man and the boy went to the car.
> Verbatim: The man, the boy he go car.

Grammatical points:
- use of connective – the man <u>and</u> . . .
- verb concordance – man + boy = they
- irregular past tense – went
- omission of connective – to?, in?
- omission of article – the or a.

- As children begin to build up a sight vocabulary an awareness of the rules for constructing a sentence can be supported by using a Breakthrough to Literacy approach to writing. The power of this can be enhanced by using colour coding according to word categories. The colour coding approach to language learning was first developed by John Lea, head teacher of Moor House School, as the Colour Pattern Scheme in the 1970s and the ideas were extended in the Language Through Reading Programme (LTR) published by Invalid Children's Aid Nationwide (ICAN). The principles of these reading schemes can be followed by combining the ideas of colour coding and Breakthrough to Literacy.
  - The child has cards with individual words which are in their sight vocabulary. Insecure words can be reinforced by pictures.
  - The words are a combination of personally important, high frequency, topic related and reading scheme words and are built up gradually over time.
  - Each word is printed in black on a coloured card. In the LTR the colours used are:
  Orange = nouns (naming words)
  Yellow = verbs (doing words)
  White = function words
  - Words of different colours are stored on different pages of the A4 word book.
  - Children construct sentences on a velcro strip and can be supported by visual cues which relate to the colour code of the words.

Alternatively, if the child is able to copy write, the sentence structure can be illustrated by coloured lines on the paper.

_____	_____	_____	etc.
black	orange	yellow	

The child selects the appropriate words, in this case

The   cat   sat . . .

The pre-preparation of text has received a new focus with the advent of the literacy hour. However, children with speech and language impairment may need to have this pre-preparation differentiated to ensure that:

- New vocabulary is explained.
- Common use vocabulary that is used in a different context so that the meaning is altered is explained.
- Complex sentences with subordinate clauses are simplified.
- The significance of connection is explained, e.g. 'At one time, but I have changed my mind, I was going to . . .'.
- The sequence of events in the text is clarified, 'John picked up his towel to go to the beach just after he fed the dog'.
  1. John fed the dog.
  2. John picked up the towel.
  3. John went to the beach.
- There is a concept of the main idea of the story. Practise thinking of a title for this paragraph or story is a very useful exercise to develop these skills.
- Inference which is important for understanding the text is explained.

Key wording

Older students who have acquired decoding skills may be supported in their understanding of a text by using the technique of **key wording**. This is a skill which will have to be taught and practised with the support of an adult before it can become a useful aid to comprehension. It is also a skill that all students may find helpful for note taking or revision.

The following is an example of key wording.

The <u>stricken submarine</u> lay at a depth of approximately twenty fathoms. Although it was common knowledge that the <u>treacherous currents</u> of the area would <u>make rescue</u> operations <u>difficult</u>, the crew remained disciplined and <u>confident</u>.

Meanwhile, outside their prison a <u>diver with</u> technical <u>equipment</u> for their release was <u>in peril</u>. His <u>life-line</u> had become <u>entangled</u> around a projection on an adjacent <u>wreckage</u>.

Task:
Can you keyword the rest of the passage?

> Experience warned him against his first impulse to dislodge the line by force. Patiently he turned and twisted. At last his calmness and persistence were rewarded. Triumphantly he detached the final loop from the obstruction. Then fatigued but undaunted by this unpleasant accident, he proceeded to provide an escape exit for the submarine's captives.

Mind mapping and visual represention

Key wording can provide the basis for mind mapping or a simple visual representation of the text.

Pre-preparation of text and key wording (Key Stages 1–4)

• A visual representation of the submarine text:

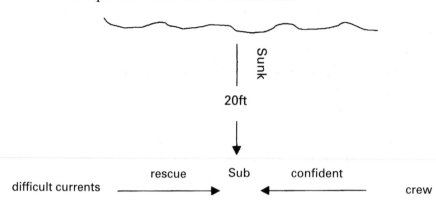

Figure 6.11

• A diagram of the text from a geography lesson:

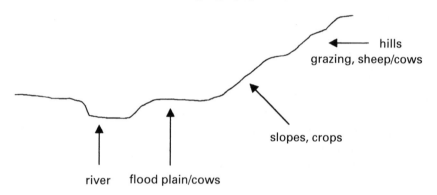

Figure 6.12

• A mind map might extend the text of the submarine or the geography lesson. Many schools are teaching mind mapping, having been inspired by reading Buzan's (1995) *Use Your Head* from BBC Books.

None of these devices needs to be a work of art, they only need to help the person who draws them to understand and remember core information. Examples of mind maps are shown in Figures 6.13a and 6.13b.

Writing frames

It is very important for teachers to have clear aims and objectives for the written tasks which they are asking children to undertake. It is equally important that they communicate these to the children in a way that provides a clear structure for the task. In this context writing frames not only help children to organise their thoughts, but also act as an 'aide memoire'.

There is a range of useful published writing frames (Lewis and Wray 1995) but those which prove most useful are frequently devised by teachers to match the tasks and the children's strengths and weaknesses. So, for example, for children with specific speech and language difficulties icons instead of words are more appropriate, or even pictures already placed in a sequence.

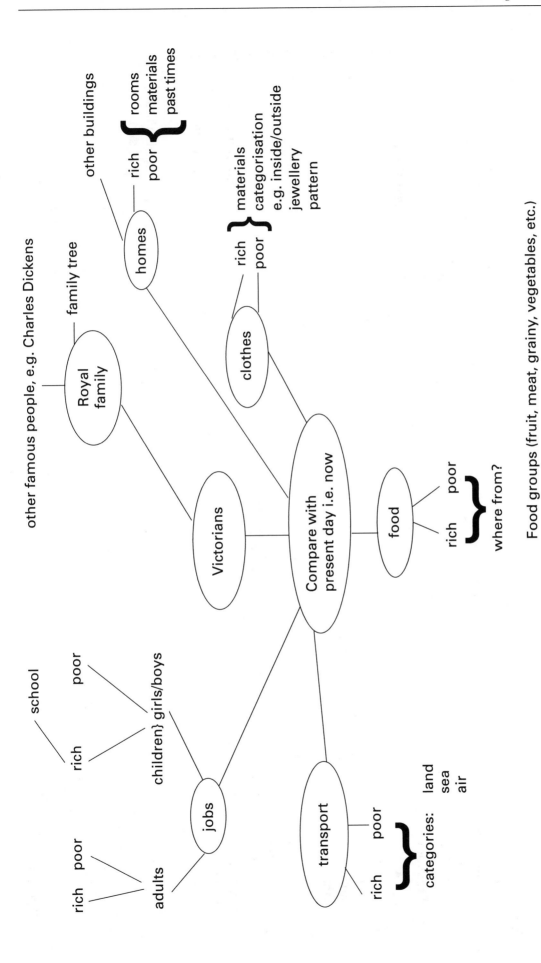

Figure 6.13a

Thanks to Louise Andrews, South Downs NHS Heath Trust

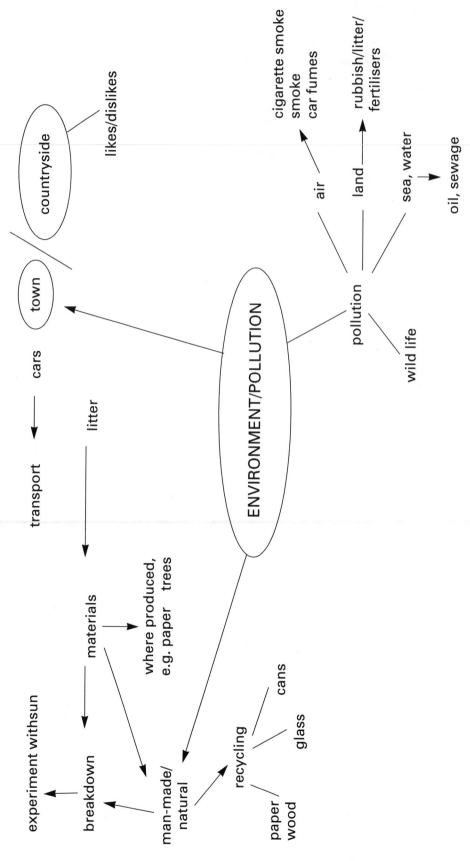

Figure 6.13b

The following are examples of useful writing frames.

'Clown frame' (Education Department of Western Australia 1989)

- This cartoon-like approach is likely to maintain the interest of the child.
- Once the child can read, icons can be replaced by words.

Introducing the News Framework

Procedure

1 Make a newstelling chart that includes *when, who, where, what, why* and *feelings*. If children have difficulty reading the key words, substitute appropriate symbols. (See illustrations below.)

2 Model how to tell news. Explain links between the information supplied and key words on the chart. Repeat the procedure a number of times until the children become skilled in identifying each element.

3 Choose children to tell news. Instruct the audience to identify elements that have been included and generate questions related to those that have been omitted. Cover key words as each is discussed.

Figure 6.14 Framework for planning news content

'Structuring creative writing' (Reproduced with the permission of South Downs Health (NHS) Trust)

1. CHARACTERS Who?	2. LOCATION Where?	3. Something starts to happen
4. The exciting bit	5. It sorts itself out (and then?)	6. The end

- Brainstorm characters and location(s). Adult writes down points.
- Brainstorm possible story lines. Adult writes ideas.
- Discuss and decide which ideas to keep/scrap. Choose a maximum of three characters.

- Brainstorm details of character and locations.
- Write first draft into boxes.
- Add detail and ensure continuity of the story line.
- Write final draft or tape record or develop into role play.

This approach is good for both individual or group work.

- The term 'Genre' (Lewis and Wray 1995).

With children who are already experiencing problems understanding vocabulary, it is not useful to use a term such as 'genre'. It would be more helpful to refer to this writing frame as writing for different purposes and for different people.

name	

date	

title	

There are differing explanations as to why/how/what/when

One explanation is that

The evidence for this is

An alternative explanation is

This explanation is based on

Of the alternative explanations I think the most likely is

Figure 6.15 Explanation genre

Chapter 7

Language and behaviour

Have you ever been lost in a strange town and stopped to ask directions? It may have been hard to 'tune-in' to a different accent or the rate and complexity of the way the directions were given may have been too overwhelming. How did you feel about having to ask for a slower, more detailed explanation, while trying to relate what was being said to landmarks you recognised or features on the map? What did you do:

- Say thank you and go away little the wiser?
- Try again, even if the person was becoming impatient with you?
- Try to ask someone else and hope they would be easier to understand?

When you returned to your car did you feel frustrated, tearful, angry or a combination of all three? Did you kick the car? Would the whole scenario have been even worse if you had had problems making yourself understood in the first place?

For children with speech and language impairment all social encounters may potentially have a similar emotional impact. It is not surprising, therefore, that children may become withdrawn or show anger and frustration about their reduced ability to communicate effectively with other people. Stevenson *et al.* (1985) showed that children who at three years of age had difficulties with language were at risk of behavioural problems at eight years. If the language problems were resolved by eight years, the risk of behavioural problems was halved.

There are several important messages to be taken from this research:

- it is important to intervene in the early years if children do have identifiable language problems;
- there is a link between delayed or disordered language development and behaviour problems;
- as the communication skills improve, the behaviour will also improve in most cases.

It is only too easy to see the surface behaviour and focus on behaviour management strategies without looking for the underlying causes of the behaviour.

Children who have problems with the understanding of language may be perceived by adults in school as being difficult or challenging.

Adult perceptions

Why might children with language problems be perceived as having seven deadly sins?

1. Naughty

- A failure to respond to requests and instructions may be seen as defiance.
- Difficulty with following the rules of the classroom and the rules of playground games may have social implications with teachers and peers.

2. Poor attention control

- Children who do not understand may cease to listen to what is being said and find other ways of occupying themselves which could be disruptive to the group.
- Children with poor listening skills may be restless during group carpet sessions such as the literacy hour, showing and telling or story time.

3. Unmotivated

- Children who have a weak auditory memory may fail to remember to bring things from home despite reminders at the end of the school day.
- Children may only remember part of what they have been asked to do or muddle instructions.

---

4. *Odd or strange*

- Children who have problems processing spoken language may respond only to key words in a question and so give off-target, unusual responses which other children may find amusing, e.g.
  Q 'Where is your brother?'
  R 'He's John.'
- Literal interpretations of idioms may result in some behaviour which appears odd, e.g.
  Teacher 'Off you go' (meaning start reading now).
  Child walks away from her.
- Auditory misperceptions may lead to some word substitutions which, again, may sound amusing to the rest of the group, e.g.
  Q 'orange, apple, banana – can you think of another one?'
  R 'tambourine' (tangerine).
  Q 'Why are you writing those lines?'
  R 'It's a puzzlement' (punishment).

5. *Liar*

- Sometimes if you have not understood the question, the easiest way out is to say 'yes'. This appears to please adults and probably passes, at least fifty per cent of the time.
- If your speech is hard to understand, it may be easier not to explain your actions but to take an easy way out and deny everything or say you did do what you were asked to do.

6. *Aggressive*

- Children who have difficulty making themselves understood will continue to attempt to control their environment by physical means long after others of their age have started to negotiate verbally.

7. *Stupid*

- Children who have unusual or unintelligible speech may be seen as stupid or be ignored by other children even at nursery/playgroup. This may become a self-fulfilling prophecy.

For children whose language follows a normal pattern of development, language becomes a substitute for action as they begin to understand better what is said to them and are able to express their needs verbally. We may expect toddlers at playgroup to snatch toys from other children but we expect an older child to say things such as 'Can I have a go?', 'Me next', 'My turn'.

Baker and Cantwell (1987) described how abnormal language development disrupts the development of the control of behaviour. They believed that children with speech and language impairment are frequently put under pressure to conform when they are unable to respond like other children. The result was all too often tantrums, behaviour problems and attention/arousal problems, all of which might be interpreted as naughty rather than as signals of stress and distress. However, they contended that the behaviour all too often became the focus of an intervention rather than the underlying cause being addressed.

There have been many studies which have shown that children with language impairments are at risk of developing emotional and behaviour problems (Conti-Ramsden and Botting 1999a, Donahue *et al.* 1994, Funk and Ruppert 1984, Gordon 1991). The positive element of the message is that the behaviour problems may subside once the language impairment has been

---

Case Study 'Introducing Derek'

By the age of four years Derek had seen many professionals who described him in their reports:

Medical officer: 'behaviour lacks control'
Social worker: 'active', 'trying', 'has he got brain damage?'
Family aid: told mother his behaviour was 'abnormal'.

The village school heard about Derek from the playgroup and from other parents. The head teacher requested a referral to the educational psychologist.
At home

- he was hard to manage – mother was on medication
- had temper tantrums 'wore his mother out'
- the family worked around avoiding upsets
- his mother did not understand his speech.

All interventions by the preschool services had focused upon managing – or attempts to manage – his behaviour until the educational psychologist referred him to the speech and language therapist.
The speech and language therapist reported that:

- comprehension age appropriate
- problems with phonology, expressive language.

Derek attended a Language Unit and joined his Village School in Y3. He did inevitably experience some literacy problems because of his early phonological problems, but behaviour was never subsequently an issue.

---

recognised and the attendant problems addressed (Funk and Ruppert).

The early warning signs of difficulties with social interactions may be apparent even at playgroup because as Hadley and Rice (1991) attested

> *Preschoolers behave as if they know who talks well and who does not, and they prefer to interact with those who do.*

Their paper describes children whose speech is hard to understand and whose grammar is poor as having fewer social interactions than other children.

This reduced opportunity to practice social communication and social skills may affect the learning of both language and social skills and it is not unusual to hear parental comments such as 'I think the others avoided him at playgroup because they did not understand what he was trying to say'.

There have been fewer studies which have focused upon the language skills of children who have already been identified as having social, emotional behavioural problems. (Beitchman *et al.* 1986, Vallance *et al.* 1999). One recent investigation (Burgess and Bransby 1990) investigated the language skills of 17 children who were in a special unit for children aged 6 to 12 years and who had emotional and behavioural difficulties. Five tests of language were administered and 16 of the 17 children were found to have speech and language difficulties for which speech and language therapy was recommended. Eleven of the children were described as having severe speech and language problems. The children did not have obvious problems with intelligibility which might have alerted professionals to their language impairment. The children were perceived as being defiant and uncooperative rather than failing to understand what was said to them and reacting to the inappropriate management of their difficulties. The unit did have behaviour management strategies but these were language based. A discussion of rules, demands for verbal explanations and 'talking' therapies are not helpful for children whose language skills are compromised.

The national agenda on the prevention of exclusions may prompt further timely research relating to students in special units for emotional, behaviour difficulties (EBD) and excluded students, to explore their language competence.

Language development and the control of behaviour

Adults attempt to control the behaviour of young children by using language in a variety of ways:

- Instructions – such as 'come on', 'hold my hand'.
- Praise – 'well done', to encourage the behaviour to be repeated.
- Admonishment – 'stop it', 'leave it alone'.
- Explanations – 'try doing it this way'.

At this stage of development, Skinner (1953) described behaviour as being under the control of others. As children develop language they begin to develop private speech and Vygotsky (1962) described the stages of the development of private speech. Vocalisations which accompany actions develop into a child talking aloud about what he/she is doing. This is commonly heard at playgroup and in Year R when children talk aloud about what they are doing in their play. Gradually this commentary develops into a plan which guides the action – 'I'm putting Teddy to bed, put on 'jamas . . .' Vygotsky argues that as speech becomes more internalised behaviour is brought increasingly under the control of language which is described as prescriptive, self-guiding speech. Eventually this speech becomes verbal thought.

Once a child is able to use self-directed private speech, behaviour ceases to be under the control of the immediate context, the here and now. It becomes rule governed, even if the rules may seem bizarre to an adult.

Language bound rules sustain behaviour over time – not running in the corridor or good sitting. They also support future goals – which may be simple such as delaying the response until the teacher asks for the answer or has finished the question, or more complex and distant such as studying for an examination.

Through the use of language, behaviour comes under conscious control, it becomes self-regulated. Thus, language is a key feature of what Barkley (1997) describes as self-regulatory behaviour which allows the mature individual to plan how to respond to a situation in a flexible, adaptable way which takes into account past experiences. The separation of feelings from action also becomes possible so that impulsive reactions such as the angry response to being told off by the boss can be withheld if we want promotion.

An idiosyncratic rule
Lines and Squares

Whenever I walk in a London street,
I'm ever so careful to watch my feet;
And I keep in the squares,
And the masses of bears,
Who wait at the corners all ready to eat
The sillies who tread on the lines of the street,
Go back to their lairs,

From: *When We Were Very Young*, A. A. Milne

Children with language problems are often described as reactive, impulsive and unable to follow the rules of the classroom. They may, therefore, frequently be misidentified as having Attention Deficit Hyperactivity Disorder (AD/HD) if the behaviour is considered without reference to the developmental profile of the child.

The children may be supported to develop the private speech which is needed to control behaviour.

Private, internalised speech

Speech uttered aloud by children that is addressed to the self or no-one in particular. *(Berk and Potts 1991)*

Vygotsky (1962) described four stages for the development of private Speech. Activities may be planned to guide children through the stages.

Only when children have reached Stage 3, do verbal strategies to control behaviour become appropriate to use. Remember – why did you do that? is not appropriate for a child who has a limited understanding of:

- a 'why' question
- cause and effect
- the language of feelings

even if they have the expressive language skills when in distress or under stress to:

- initiate a response
- organise the word order for a sentence
- use the construct why–because
- access the words needed to express feelings.

In a paper with the title 'Baby looks very sad', Denham (1992) and her colleagues studied how mothers talk to their toddlers about feelings and what might make people feel sad or happy or any other emotion. These early discussions help children to learn the meaning of the labels we apply to emotions (e.g. jealous, angry), to link these to events in their lives and the lives of their family and to match the 'emotion words' to non-verbal signals such as facial expression, tone of voice or body language. The early learning of the language of emotions helps children later in life to recognise the emotions of others and by reading the signals accurately to manage social

Stage 1 ⟶	Group practical activity such as colouring/sticking. Encourage vocalisations about the shared activity using the appropriate names for objects and processes. Conversation about preferred topics while engaged on simple tasks.
Stage 2 ⟶	Small group practical activity, including maths, science activities. Children describe what they are doing using appropriate verbs, nouns, adverbs, adjectives. Answer simple cause and effect questions and task relevant questions. Recap and recall the sequence of actions and the outcomes. Verbal commentary accompanies actions.
Stage 3 ⟶	Small group activity. Facilitator encourages the use of language to plan the task – equipment needed – the process/sequence – timing for the elements – outcomes – evaluations.
Stage 4 ⟶	Facilitator encourages children to verbalise their problem solving, but in their heads. They may still verbalise out loud when the task is difficult. At this stage the children should be able to use language to explain what was done and why when asked.

encounters more successfully. Missing out on this early learning because of delayed or disordered language development may have long-term effects upon social and emotional development.

Dunn and Brown (1991) suggested that children who are going through this learning process at three years, are better able to predict at aged six years how others might feel and react when presented with tasks which involve social cognition. A level of language competence is, therefore, an important factor in the development of **emotional literacy**.

The non-verbal aspects of communication can be as important as the words themselves. We may not always be aware of how carefully we monitor facial expression when we are talking to someone except if they suddenly give a strong signal such as a frown. Our reliance upon non-verbal signals may become apparent when we are met with a blank, unresponsive gaze which gives us no feedback about how our message is being received. This sometimes happens with dyspraxic children who have difficulty with signalling using facial expression or, perhaps, with autistic children who have not developed this subtle form of social communication.

The lack of feedback tends to make us feel uncomfortable so that we may break off the conversation and even avoid that person in the future. This reliance on non-verbal feedback develops early in life, as shown by the work of Walden and Field (1990) with preschool children. The children were asked to rate others on a sociometric preference questionnaire. The most popular preschoolers were those who were best able to signal their feelings with facial expression and to discriminate the expressions of other children. Similarly, Spence (1987) found that children aged three to five years liked best those peers who were good at interpreting facial expression and understanding how others might feel in familiar situations.

All these studies support the idea of Dodge (1996) who suggested a social information-processing model of social competence. This means that, the more a child understands about the verbal and non-verbal language of feelings, the more likely he/she is to read the social signals of peers appropriately and react in a way that the others find rewarding. Their own ability to signal feeling by using facial expression helps others to respond appropriately in their turn. A well-managed encounter has a high probability of being judged rewarding and is, therefore, more likely to be repeated.

Children who have good social communication skills at an early age are popular among their peers. This reputation often endures because status is continually reinforced and confirmed by the group with positive conse-quences for self-image and self-esteem. For children with low status the reverse is the case (Figure 7.1).

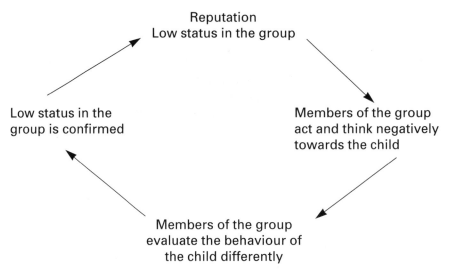

Figure 7.1

Students with less severe difficulties may have been included in games and friendship groups with their peers at primary school where proximity, energy levels and shared physical activities are still relatively important in choosing friends. However, even these students may become more at risk in the changing social context of a secondary school. At the Secondary phase of education quick-fire verbal interactions which may take the form of jokes, adolescent slang and puns which depend on understanding ambiguity become increasingly important in defining group membership. The complexities of the non-literal use of language, the use of implied language to convey meaning and the verbal subtleties which may influence the forming and re-forming of friendship groups may leave the student with speech and language impairment vulnerable and confused. The reduced ability to 'defend' themselves verbally may trigger physical aggression or result in them becoming a victim of teasing or more severe bullying (see Case Study at end of Chapter 1). Among adolescent girls in particular, talking through feelings, discussing relationships and predicting the behaviours of others, is often the 'glue' which binds friendships and these are not skills which girls with speech and language impairment will use with fluency.

Teachers may not always be aware that a student in their class has speech and language impairment and the student's response may easily give rise to misperceptions.

Teachers and administrators have difficulty making distinctions between a 'can't' and a 'won't' attitude and students often suffer the consequences of what appears to be non-compliance and stubbornness.

(Freedman and Willig 1995)

The behaviours which speech and language impaired students show – reluctant attendance, work avoidance, losing books, etc. – are the very behaviours that are taken by teachers to indicate low motivation and disinterest (Moats and Lyon 1993).

The girl described in the Case Study at the end of Chapter 1 was perceived as 'a bit sulky' because she did not respond to conversational overtures from her teachers. A Year 9 boy was perceived to respond in an off-hand rather 'rude' way because of his short rather defensive answers to questions. His difficulties organising expressive language and word-finding difficulties made any question and answer session very anxiety provoking and, therefore, a situation he was keen to avoid if possible. Other students may automatically say 'yes' when asked if they have understood what has been said and then fail to act appropriately. It is often then assumed, either that they have not listened or that they are being deliberately uncooperative. The girl in the Case Study said that she had at one time asked her teachers when she did not understand, but successive repeats were often no easier for her to follow so she eventually stopped asking because teachers began to show irritation if she kept on 'pestering' them.

It is important that the adults who work with these students model appropriate behaviour such as:

- giving the student time to compose a response and offering supportive prompts;
- simplifying the language they use with the student;
- providing opportunities for the student to show areas of skill and competence within the class group.

In conclusion, there is a strong body of evidence which shows that children who have experienced delayed or disordered language development are at risk for developing behaviour problems. A reduced ability to understand what others want of them and/or a reduced ability to explain what they need and want is in itself a source of frustration to the individual. The consequent behaviour is open to misinterpretation by the adults and other children that they encounter. The way in which other people react and respond to us shapes the behaviour that we show towards them. The reactions and signals of others is a key element in the development of our self-image and self-esteem. Children with speech and language impairment are at risk of developing poor self-image and low self-esteem. Parents and teachers need to be aware of this and find as many opportunities as possible to build the self-esteem of children with speech and language impairment. Language impaired children are the same as anyone else in this respect. In addition to the direct consequences of the language impairment, the children's ability to monitor and control their behaviour may be affected by their reduced ability to develop what Vygotsky called internalised speech.

The development of social skills is also mediated by the use of language. The effects of being less able to use verbal and non-verbal communication skills may begin to show, even at preschool in terms of popularity among peers and there may be long-term consequences of early rejection or isolation.

Peer relationships play an important role in emotional, social, academic and behavioural development.

- It is in this context that new social skills are acquired and existing ones refined and elaborated.
- They provide emotional support and the models for behaviour.
- They are the prototypes for subsequent relationships.

Children who do not enjoy the support of their peers are at further risk for developing low self-esteem, and later mental health problems.

The positive message is that using strategies which are now well established in many schools, can make a difference. These strategies would include: Buddy systems, Circle of Friends, and interventions such as social skill training which is planned to meet the specific needs of small groups of children.

Chapter 8

Social groups

There are two types of social situation which occur regularly in schools and which may cause particular difficulties for a child who has speech and language problems; working and playing as a member of a group.

For most children the social relationships and social skills which they experiment with first in play are a valuable preparation for working as a member of a group. Children who have not previously had successful group experiences are at a disadvantage before the group begins to attempt a task. Even for children who do have background experience of the relevant social skills, Johnson and Johnson (1989) offer the reminder that,

Social groups in the classroom and on the playground

Working as a member of a group

Putting children into groups, setting a task and telling them to cooperate does not necessarily promote cooperation and achievement.

There are four different types of work groups which are routinely set up in the classroom. Two of the groups do not involve cooperation beyond sharing any equipment held in common and participating in any social interaction which is tolerated by the teacher. In these groups, although the children may choose to talk about topics related to the task, or not, discussion and interaction are not integral to what is happening.

Examples of non-cooperative groups

1. **Unrelated tasks with an individual product**	Children sit around a table all working on different parts of a maths scheme
2. **Identical task with an individual product**	Children sit around table all writing their news

These group activities may not present particular problems provided that the tasks or the task outcomes are appropriately differentiated.

The other two groups do involve a degree of cooperation and collaboration;

Examples of cooperative groups

1. **Jigsaw elements with a joint outcome**	Children all cut and stick a figure for a collage which is the product of the group
2. **Joint task, joint outcome**	Children are asked to solve a science problem by experimentation and report back to the whole class

Children with a speech and language impairment may be quite comfortable sitting at a table following their own activities which are differentiated by input or output to meet their needs. If any of the equipment is shared, they may have difficulty asking for items by name in an appropriate way, timing their requests and waiting their turn. These social aspects of working alongside other children may need some direct teaching, the modelling of appropriate language and behaviour and adult support before a child is able to be fully independent.

Cooperative group work is a difficult experience for many children with speech and language impairment so they all too easily opt out and become watchers rather than participants. The skills which are involved in collaborative working involve:

- listening to the contributions of other children;
- waiting for a turn to speak;
- thinking about what other people have said and avoiding topic hopping;
- stating your own ideas clearly;
- clarifying your ideas, and an ability to 'repair' the conversation, if that is needed;

- negotiation if there is a problem or a difference of opinion;
- accepting constructive criticism and the modification of your ideas by others.

These are all quite sophisticated aspects of verbal communication which most children will develop gradually through the primary phase of their education.

In addition to being 'stuck' at an earlier phase of their language development than their peers, children with speech and language impairment may have difficulties with the pragmatic aspects of their use of language:

- how to initiate a contribution;
- how to turn-take in a conversation;
- how to time interventions;
- how to end a contribution;
- avoiding violations of style in terms of the words they choose, the volume, pitch and rhythms of speech;
- maintaining a social distance which is comfortable to others in the group (proxemics).

A degree of emotional maturity is also required of group members who may become upset or angry if their idea is not the one chosen or praised by the teacher or the other members of the group.

It is hard for children, particularly those with low self-esteem, to accept even constructive criticism of their idea or their product. Ideas for improvement may be interpreted as a total rejection and the selection of an idea or a design which is not theirs for adoption by the group may be a trigger for tears or tantrums.

Working as a member of a cooperative group can be made more accessible for any children with special needs by providing a structure for the group.

The establishment of structure within the group supports the learning process. *(Topping 1992)*

Ideas for structuring a group might include:

- **The allocation of roles** – Each member of the group is given a role which they are best able to fill. The roles might be that of scribe, reader of instructions, collector of equipment, chairperson.

  For most groups, the roles would rotate between the members of the group so that everyone has a turn but some roles may not be appropriate for children with speech and language impairment unless there is an adult to support them to generalise a skill which they have been learning as a specific social communication target.

- **The allocation of tasks** – Each member of the group makes a contribution to the joint goal which is complementary to other tasks. For example, to make a collage connected to a history topic different children might research costume or domestic interiors, cut, colour, write captions . . . A child who has strong visual-spatial skills, despite their speech and language impairment, might be well placed to make a contribution which could raise their esteem among the peer group.

Playing as a member of a group

The work of Baker and Cantwell (1987) demonstrated how children who have speech and language problems rely on physical means to regulate social encounters for longer than children who are able to use language to negotiate a turn or ask for a toy. Physical, rough and tumble play, may also persist when other children have moved on to more sophisticated rule-based games which are mediated by language. On the playground, in particular, they may be perceived as immature and/or aggressive because of the ways in which they attempt to interact with the other children. Playground supervisors need to be made aware that they will find it hard to:

- ask for a toy or other equipment;
- ask for a turn and negotiate a turn;
- ask to join in with a game;
- negotiate rules or a role in a game;
- understand the verbal rules that others make up and may even be modified as the game proceeds;
- respond to verbal teasing or banter without resorting to a physical response.

Short-term strategies

If problems do arise on the playground, there are some strategies which will help the child to understand:

- give a short simple rule, e.g. 'No hitting';
- reinforce the message with a sign or a visual symbol;
- remind the child of the target (all children of their targets) before they go out to play using the visual symbol for reference;
- change the target as appropriate;
- avoid long discussions about 'why': 'Why' is a complex concept which developmentally is understood after the other 'wh' questions. Where?, What?, Who?, are mastered first and then When? – a difficult time concept. Why? involves an understanding of the grammatical construction 'Why–because'. A child with expressive language problems may not have the skills to give an explanation, particularly when under stress or in distress. A failure to respond may be misunderstood as defiance rather than an inability to produce the language which is required in order to respond;
- avoid discussions which involve feelings: a child with speech and language impairment may have a very insecure understanding of the language of feelings as explained in the papers by Denham (1992) and Dunn and Brown (1991). 'Happy' and 'sad' may be the only 'feelings' words that young children with speech and language impairment do understand. A commonly asked question such as 'How do you think _____ feels because you did that?' is clearly inappropriate at many levels, even if it is a genuine question.

Long-term planning

A more long-term strategy to support children at playtime might involve careful observation about what has gone wrong. The child is unlikely to be able to tell you in words about the situation which led to a confrontation and so observation of the setting, the triggers (antecedents) and the pay off (consequences) of the behaviour is the best way to proceed. The results from the observations should help with the three elements in behaviour management, as described by La Vigna *et al.* 1989.

- **Changes to the environment** – How can the situations which give rise to conflicts be avoided?
- **New skills** – What new skills does the child need to learn in order to manage the trigger situation more successfully? New skills such as asking 'Can I play?' might be taught in role play and play scripts within a structured setting before asking a child to generalise the skill by trying it out on the playground with an adult to facilitate the interaction. A child who does not have the necessary verbal skills might use signs or symbols which are introduced also to the other children on the playground.
- **Coping strategies** – Sometimes, while new skills are being taught and before they are generalised, coping strategies have to be employed. An example of a coping strategy might be for the child to join in an adult facilitated game or activity. This may have the advantage of providing an opportunity for structured practice of the new skills which are being taught and are emerging.

Chapter 9

Inclusion and working with parents

Most children by the time they enter school have a well-developed understanding and use of language and their speech is almost completely intelligible. However, children with speech and language impairment can have very limited and/or an unusual understanding of language, of how words are put together to express ideas and feelings and can be completely unintelligible.

The importance of a planned introduction to the school for a pupil with significant speech and language difficulties cannot be overemphasised. This applies whether the child is joining the nursery or reception class at the normal point of entry, or whether the child is transferring to a new school environment.

The majority of children with speech and language difficulties are educated within the framework of mainstream education with only a minority requiring the more long-term support of a specialist school. Legislation dating back more than 20 years, has promoted the right of children with special needs to receive their education with their peers. The most recent government document, *Excellence for All Children* (the DfEE 1997 Green Paper), further supports this by introducing the notion of 'inclusion', which requires schools to respond to all pupils by reconsidering curricular organisation, rather than focusing purely on the needs of one individual child which can be described as integration. Parents of children with speech and language difficulties understandably express concerns regarding the ability of schools to meet the needs of their children. Do they have the specialist knowledge needed to teach the child and at the same time provide appropriate intervention to resolve the child's specific speech and language difficulty?

The concept of integration is based upon the idea of a 'Readiness Model' (Lipsky and Gartner 1997) which suggests/proposes that the child can only join a mainstream setting when their skills have been sufficiently developed. There is, therefore, an expectation that the child must change rather than the curriculum being changed for the child.

Summary

Integration: Suggests that the child must change in order to learn with his/her mainstream peers

Inclusion: Suggests that the school reconsiders and restructures the teaching and learning processes, pupil groupings and the use of available support for learning in order to respond to the needs of *all* pupils

---

Case Study 'An example of good practice'

When Gemma entered Greenfields Primary School she had limited understanding of spoken language and was using three-word sentences. She found following routines extremely difficult and at times became distressed and frustrated when she was unable to understand and express herself.

On the advice of her speech and language therapist, Gemma's teacher provided visual prompts to support her learning throughout the day. For example, she introduced a visual timetable to provide structure and predictability to Gemma's day. Also for each activity Gemma was given prompt cards to remind her of the equipment she would need. The teacher noticed that these strategies were also useful for other children and so employed them as part of regular classroom organisation. A year later when Bobby entered the class, with a range of learning difficulties, he was immediately able to benefit from this inclusive approach which by this time had been adopted by all Key Stage 1 teachers in the school.

Working in partnership with parents

Parents have become very aware of how they and the school need to be working in partnership, in order effectively to meet the needs of their children.

The following is a list of suggestions for schools working with parents of pupils with speech and language difficulties.

- It helps when schools keep in mind that the parents of pupils with speech and language difficulties will probably have experienced periods of considerable stress related to the management of their children. Any transition such as entering school is particularly stressful.
- It is helpful for schools to understand that where pupils have significant speech and language difficulties, these parents will almost certainly have had to argue and negotiate for resources and support. Finding the appropriate educational provision will not have been as straightforward as it is for many other parents. An understanding approach by the school is helpful in these circumstances.
- It is important that schools welcome parents and maintain good contact with them from the outset.
- Schools need to be sensitive in the ways that they communicate with parents to avoid implying fault or blame. Parents may have experienced the judgemental and negative reactions of others long before their child started attending school.
- Parents do not find it easy to hear that their child is causing concern at school. They need to be prepared for the news that the school is experiencing some difficulties or is seeking the help of outside agencies. If regular contact is maintained with the parents, there will be no surprises.
- Communication in the form of a home–school liaison book or diary offers parents reassurance and speed of contact.
- It helps for schools to be very specific about the amount and nature of support being provided for their child in school. Discussions about Individual Education Plans (IEPs) will provide a vehicle for this.
- The opportunity for parents to meet regularly with school staff to discuss their child's progress should be part of the school's approach to all children with special needs, which includes those with significant speech and language difficulties.
- Schools should be willing to seek advice and support from outside agencies such as speech and language therapists when necessary, after consultation with parents.
- All staff should be included in speech and language awareness training. Everyone working with the child needs to be aware of his/her difficulties. Much of the positive work undertaken by the class teachers can be undone when an incident is badly handled in the playground, or at dinnertime, by ill-informed staff. It is important to raise whole-school awareness.
- Offering parents the contact name and address of support groups enables parents to feel included and well supported.
- When pupils with speech and language difficulties become teenagers, they can become acutely aware of their social isolation, which can lead to depression and anxiety. This is a key time for parents and school to work together on strategies to alleviate the difficulties experienced by the pupils.

- Parents are aware that there are children with other special needs in the school and that teachers only have a limited time to spend with one child. It helps when schools understand the depth of anxiety that parents can feel on behalf of their very vulnerable child.
- Discussions between parents and teachers need to be confidential and private. Schools should therefore provide a suitable venue to accommodate these requirements. Parents can feel very awkward about sharing information and hearing feedback given to them in the presence of other parents.
- Parents appreciate receiving positive feedback about their child from teachers. It is helpful to know that schools are focusing on their child's strengths and positive behaviour. Parents are always pleased to hear about their child's success or how he/she has been included by the other children in their activities.

Preparing for successful inclusion at times of transition

Pupils of all ages may be afraid, frustrated or angry during periods of transition, which are always stressful and unsettling. They can face ridicule, contempt, teasing, and even bullying, because despite their best efforts to conform and make the right responses their difficulties with communication will betray them as being different.

The importance of a planned introduction to the school for pupils with speech and language difficulties cannot be overemphasised. This applies whether the child is joining the nursery or reception class or transferring to a new school environment. Much can be gained by following steps 1 to 4 which follow.

Step 1: A meeting of the key people. This should include:

- Key school staff – class teacher, SENCO and head at primary level; form tutor, SENCO and year head at secondary level.
- Key school staff from the previous school or from preschool provision.
- Professionals concerned, e.g. speech and language therapist, educational psychologist, social worker.
- Parents.
- Occasionally the pupil themselves if appropriate.

The meeting should:

- Identify the pupil's strengths and areas of difficulty.
- Share information on successful and unsuccessful strategies used to date.
- Plan for any changes that will be inherent in the new school environment.
- Plan for the introduction of the pupil to the new school environment.
- Identify the key person in school who will be responsible for helping the child to settle into school and for liaising with other members of staff.

Step 2: A staff development session to raise awareness of speech and language difficulties. This should include all staff involved in working with the child. Particular attention should be given to informing and supporting staff who will supervise the child during unstructured periods of the day such as lunchtimes, since these can be very difficult for children with speech and language difficulties. The staff session should cover:

- A detailed description of the child's speech and language difficulties.
- How the child's difficulties are affecting his/her learning and behaviour.
- How best to help the pupil.
- How to help the other pupils support the young person with speech and language difficulties.
- Sources of literature, references, video material, etc.
- Identifying the link support person for the child.

The training should be given by one or several professionals who have expertise in the area of speech and language difficulties and, preferably, who know the child.

Step 3: A plan of what to say to the other pupils. Pupils with speech and language difficulties often have problems with interpersonal and social skills.

- It is helpful for other pupils to understand why the child is different and how they can help.
- If they are willing and available parents can be profitably involved in this process.
- Pupils with speech and language difficulty are frequently open to exploitation, e.g. to be told by another child to tell X he is stupid. Pupils and young people need to understand that this behaviour is a form of bullying.
- Always emphasise the child's strengths and skills.
- Enlist the help of older pupils to keep a watchful eye on the pupil with speech and language difficulties at playtime/lunchtimes.

Step 4: Introducing the pupil to the school. The pressures experienced by all pupils entering new schools are far more stressful for those with speech and language difficulties. Particular pressures are:

- Unpredictable demands.
- Differing expectations.
- Being part of a large group of children.
- Finding his/her way around the school.
- Following a timetable (for older children).

The following can prove most helpful and should be considered:

- Where possible the pupil with speech and language difficulties should visit the school out of school hours in order to familiarise him/herself with the layout of the school.
- Ensure that the pupil knows where to sit and where to keep his/her possessions (tray, peg, etc.).
- It is important to use visual approaches in the classroom, e.g. visual timetable.
- School rules need to be presented in a way that makes them accessible in the classroom and it is helpful for the pupil to have the opportunity to share these at home with their parents.

- Familiarise the pupil with those members of staff to whom he/she can turn in times of difficulty.
- When pupils are able to read, any information they need to be aware of can be written down.

A sample of mothers was interviewed in order to elicit their opinions on the way they and their children had been dealt with by the health and education systems. The problems experienced by their children were across the spectrum of speech and language impairment, from severe receptive language difficulties to expressive language difficulties and severe phonological problems.

The first question covered their recollections of the period of time when school placement was being sorted out/discussed.

Before starting school *(Interview schedule, see Appendix 3)*
Only one mother expressed deep concern about what might happen to her child as she and her husband were still only becoming aware of the severity of their child's difficulties and the possible long-term implications of them. She said,

> *'It was pretty apparent that if he went into an ordinary mainstream class, he wouldn't be able to cope, he wouldn't be able to communicate and he wouldn't be on the receiving end of communication either. I just didn't know what the education provision could be for him. We looked at the local primaries and rejected them. Basically, they were awfully nice to us when we went round, but they really didn't want to touch us with a bargepole.'*

The other parents already had their children in specialist preschool placements or were receiving intensive speech and language therapy at the local clinic. One mother had already been briefed regarding the various educational placements available. She realised that for her child the best provision would be in a Speech and Language Unit, which was part of a local mainstream school. She said,

> *'I knew it would be the best place for him and it was a question of praying and fingers crossed. It was a really stressful period but all the way through I was helped by the professionals and spoke to some other mothers. It was exactly as it should be.'*

Another mother admitted that she was not really so aware of the severity of her child's difficulties and therefore had no concerns about her attending school. She admitted,

> *'Although I did notice the problem, I didn't take too much notice because I was all wrapped up in having lost a daughter the year before. She was receiving lots of help from R at the Child Development Centre so I wasn't so worried.'*

Another mother was rather horrified when the possibility of special provision was mentioned. Her immediate reaction was one of rejection:

What parents said about the system, professionals and inclusion

'I was horrified and really didn't think F was bad enough. The location was a huge problem, it wasn't a local school involved, and I found it impossible to cope with the idea of placing my son in a taxi to go to a Language Unit at another school. I actually thought it would be full of foreign children who couldn't speak English. I discussed it with my friends at the mother and toddlers group and they thought I was mad to turn down the possibility of a small class with all that specialist help, so I started to think logically and decided this would be best for him. When it came to L, I was so convinced he needed the Unit, I was prepared to refuse to send him to school.' (This mother has three of her four children with severe and specific language impairment.)

The second question concerned the transition period **Starting School** *(see Appendix 3)*

One child attended her local mainstream school and her mother was very satisfied with the way the staff dealt with her problems. When it was suggested that she needed to have a Statement of Special Educational Needs, it was only then that she realised the extent of her daughter's difficulty. She admitted,

'When I got the report I was gob-smacked, I hadn't realised before then it was such a major problem. I wasn't thinking ahead, just taking each day as it came. When I read it, I was horrified, I thought this isn't my daughter, you've got it wrong, and I cried. I was horrified. Eventually, it all sunk in and I realised that I must take the advice. I shall always be grateful to you all for making me think.'

The other mothers confided that their children all experienced major problems settling into the Language Unit on the first day. One child bit the teacher in the arm but eventually settled down. The other children both had major tantrums, but with the behaviour policies in place in class they eventually became more compliant. One mother said,

'I found it incredibly difficult to cope with the changes and we had a lot of behavioural difficulties with him; lying on the floor, screaming and not wanting to do anything he was asked to do. Unfortunately, or perhaps fortunately, because the school had such a structure we had a bit of a rebound effect at home. Suddenly he used up all of his ability to be compliant during the day, so that it was pretty hairy at home. I put a lot of it down to tiredness and we somehow got through it, but it was wonderful that every school night he went to bed and went to sleep. He'd been made to use his considerable brain power all day at school.'

This particular mother was very clear about what she remembered most of this period.

'It was J realising that all the adults in his universe were wise to him and he couldn't manipulate them, he couldn't get away with it any longer. I can remember feeling a sense of glee and thinking it was rather humourous – it was lovely – you do need a sense of humour by you when you've got a child with language difficulties anyway, but it was really great. It was really wonderful to feel that something was at last being done for him and was going to unlock his ability and his ability to communicate. It was really a tremendous relief.'

The parents were asked about the children's **current provision** *(see Appendix 3, questions 3 and 4)*, either Language Unit or mainstream class, and for those whose children had transferred from Language Unit to mainstream class full time their recollections of that period. For one mother the transition from Language Unit to mainstream class presented no difficulties, although when the subject was first discussed she admitted to feeling very unsure:

> *'I did wonder whether she'd cope, would the teacher understand H's problems and be able to cope with them. Then I thought, she must have had this before, but then I thought they're there (the staff of the Language Unit) if there's a problem, they'll sort it out.'*

H transferred to a mainstream class in the host school, which her mother felt, eased the transition and H coped extremely well.

Another mother felt the process had gone well but was just a bit too soon for her son. She feels fortunate that her local school had an excellent SENCO at the time who was also her child's class teacher. Subsequent years have not gone so well mainly, she feels, because it was the policy of the school that each new teacher 'discovered' a child's strengths and weaknesses before reading the file. Equally, parents were not invited to meet the teacher until the end of the first term. She was most disillusioned to be told,

> *'F's English is letting him down',*

and when challenged the teacher agreed she had not read the file. This mother was further alarmed when the same scenario was repeated a year later. Of her two other children with language difficulties, one was in a Language Unit and making excellent progress, although she was extremely concerned about transition to secondary school. She feels he will not cope without a specialist facility at a mainstream school. Her youngest son is currently in a mainstream class and she said of him,

> *'A's education suffered dreadfully because he didn't go to a Language Unit. The school were convinced at first that he was just a very naughty boy. Unfortunately, he'd latched on to the naughtiest boy in the school.'*

She admitted that since a change of head teacher things had improved at the school for both of the boys, and that at present their language difficulties were acknowledged and being addressed.

Two mothers whose children were still in Language Units both expressed satisfaction at the progress of their children. One said,

> *'If people had said to me two years ago that he would be coming out of the other end of this system now and going into a mainstream school full time, I wouldn't have believed them because I knew he had so much ground to cover.'*

She continued,

> *'When the move was discussed with us I thought, oh no, the prospect of him not having this wonderfully inclusive and welcoming environment and having to go and sink or swim in a big class, was quite daunting. However, once we realised how much help he'd get during transition, and we'd found the right school with the right attitude, we were thrilled to think he was going.'*

All the parents voiced their concerns on how being in a large mainstream class full time would impact on their children's self-esteem. All of the children but one had experienced major problems with self-esteem. One parent summed up the difficulties,

> *'It has taken so long to get him feeling good about himself, but a wrong word or mishandled situation could undo years of hard and patient work.'*

The next question *(see question 5)* addressed the possible **impact of communication impairments upon relationships**.

Several parents commented on the stress in their own relationship as a result of their child's communication problem. In general, the mothers felt that the burden of the everyday management of their children had fallen on their shoulders and although their partners were supportive, they were not always understanding of the emotional traumas being experienced by the mother. One mother said,

> *'Having to deal with it day to day, especially when you're not sure what's really wrong, you need a shoulder to cry on – you need somebody to be a sounding board. I felt it was me against the world.'*

Similarly, grandparents, friends, and people in the supermarket were not always understanding. One mother commented,

> *'I think the other thing that people don't allow for, when you have a child with difficulties, is the amount of criticism both covert and overt that you get. I can remember being very distressed at people within the family and outside making remarks about the lack of discipline, about how his behaviour was totally unacceptable, and trying to fight the corner of how do you discipline a child who doesn't understand what you're asking him to do.'*

Several mothers recollected their feelings of loss and bereavement. One said,

> *'I wouldn't blame anybody for becoming deeply depressed. I went through it and I did myself. In a sense it's a grief process, a process of bereavement.'*

Another mother summed up a shared theme,

> *'S is a twenty-four hours a day, seven days a week child – it is such hard work having to break everything down so he understands. It can be hard going and sometimes you can't help it, you just get cross.'*

One mother explained how having three children with severe speech and language difficulties had helped her understanding of her husband's language problems. She said,

> *'If I hadn't learned about language difficulties through the children, I don't think we'd be together now. He always carries his camera with him and takes 'photos. It drove me mad.'*

Also,

> *'he has severe word-finding difficulties and I could never understand why he found it so hard to express his feelings and aspirations.'*

All the parents expressed their concern over how the other children in the family had 'lost out' in terms of time and attention. The effect of having a child with speech and language impairment on other siblings had been different for different families. One mother said,

> *'It has made them more understanding and tolerant in the long run of all people with disabilities.'*

For another it was the opposite because one sibling was not understanding of the younger one,

> *'will stay there until it comes to fisticuffs.'*

For some of the children friendships with their peers can still be a problem, but this was certainly not the case for all. One mother commented,

> *'We are isolated (the family live in a house in the country) and understandably no one wanted to play with a little boy who hit them and had tantrums.'*

But another said,

> *'When she went to the mainstream full time she made a really good friend and they're still joined at the hip, they are!'*

The responses to **'what would you say to professionals?'** *(question 6)* correlated strongly with the previously positive or negative experiences of the parents. One parent said,

> *'I haven't a bad word to say about all the help, all the support I've been given. On the other hand, for other people, not just for S, when I hear of all the children coming through with his sort of problems, there should be more of you.'*

Another commented,

> *'I would really say look at that child and see all the potential there is and then work to unlock it. Don't dismiss a child because they can't speak and can't understand.'*

From yet another mother,

> *'Those aware of language problems have been excellent and always steered me in the right direction, even when I didn't agree, but most teachers in mainstream school are not the same – they don't have the same understanding. I have not always been understood and, worse, not believed. I try not to be critical and not be judgemental but sometimes I just want to hit them on the nose!'*

The question on **inclusion** *(question 7)* evoked varied responses. However, one mother summarised the feelings of all:

> *'Every child should have the opportunity to be included, but J would have experienced hell at first being in an ordinary mainstream class and it would not have been fair to either him or the teacher. In the Language Unit he has been included in so many things in the mainstream and yet has had the specialist teaching and therapy he so desperately needed. It's not like he's been put out there in a hut somewhere with the others on their own. The unit is very much part of the school and without it he would never be taking his place in an ordinary mainstream class full time. I believe that inclusion is a process that takes place over time.'*

Terminology

Phonology – The way in which sounds are organised in language to convey differences of meaning. The study of the sound systems of language.

Articulation – The way in which we make sounds for speech; the coordination and sequencing of the fine and rapid movements necessary for the production of sounds and sound sequences.

Semantics – Handling the meaning of words and sentences; expressing meaningful ideas that reflect what is going on, and understanding other people's expression of ideas.

Use, also known as Pragmatics – Knowing the social functions of language – that is, being able to sense when to joke, when to explain things at length, and when to use different kinds of language for different situations and relationships.

Grammar – The structural organisation of a language.

Morphology – The study of the structure or form of words.

Syntax – Traditional term for the study of the rules governing the way in which words are combined to form sentences in a language.

Morpheme – The minimal distinctive unit of grammar.

Discourse – A continuous medium for the transmission of language.

Speech – The spoken medium for the transmission of language.

Metalinguistic abilities – Involves a conscious awareness of language. Our abilities as mature language users to reflect and consciously manipulate the rules of our language system.

Brief notes on assessments often used by speech and language therapists with school aged children

The Bankson Language Test (Bankson, N.W. 1990)

Objectives:	Looks at understanding and/or use of language in three areas: semantics (content), morphology/syntax (form) and pragmatics (use).
Age range:	3–7 years.
Equipment/Presentation:	Child responds to questions/instructions, some involving pictures.
Strengths:	Results give indication of main areas of difficulty. Can be used for comprehension or expression. A short screen test also included.
Weaknesses:	Lengthy. Americanised picture and verbal material.
Type of result:	Percentile scores.

Boehm Test of Basic Concepts (Boehm, R. 1983, revised 1988)

Objectives:	A test of concept knowledge.
Age range:	5–7 years.
Equipment/Presentation:	Child is given booklet containing a number of sets of pictures. Tester asks child to indicate picture corresponding to concept/word given.
Strengths:	A preschool version available. Easy to administer to one or group of children.
Weaknesses:	Some pictures not clear. Reliance on two-dimensional presentation of concepts such as prepositions.
Type of result:	Percentile.

British Picture Vocabulary Scale, 2nd edn 1997 (Dunn, L. M., Whetton, C. and Burley, J.)

Objectives:	A test of word knowledge, from concrete nouns and verbs through to abstract concepts and adjectives.
Age range:	3–18 years.
Equipment/Presentation:	Child is shown a series of pages showing four black and white line drawings. Child points to the picture showing the word given by the tester.
Strengths:	Has a short and long version to suit children's attention spans, or when time is limited. Easy to administer.

Weaknesses:	Children can use a process of elimination to achieve a correct response, even if they do not know the word (although this is a useful skill too!).
Type of result:	Age equivalent and percentile.

The Bus Story (Renfrew, C. 1994 2nd edn)

Objective:	To assess child's ability to produce consecutive speech, in order to analyse sentence strength and complexity, as well as vocabulary.
Age range:	3–8 years.
Equipment/Presentation:	A picture book shows the story of a naughty bus. The tester tells the story, according to a script then asks the child to retell the story, using the pictures to prompt. The response is tape recorded then transcribed for analysis.
Strengths:	Assesses the ability to use a connected narrative. Easy to administer and analyse.
Weaknesses:	Story a little 'childish' for older children.
Type of result:	Age equivalent for sentence length, number of complex sentences and information (vocabulary) given.

Clinical Evaluation of Language Fundamentals (CELF) (Semel, E., Wing, E., Secord, W. 1980)

Objectives:	A number of sub-tests look at ability across a range of receptive language and processing skills.
Age range:	5–16 years.
Equipment/Presentation:	Child is asked to respond to questions, instructions and examples of language given by the tester. Sub-tests can be used without administering whole test. Whole test is comprehensive. UK and preschool versions available. Linked to a range of worksheets relating to difficulties shown by test.
Strengths:	Especially useful with other children and teenagers. Gives seperate expressive/receptive results, and insights into underlying skills.
Weaknesses:	Whole test lengthy to administer.
Type of results:	Standard scores and percentiles for sub-tests and overall.

Derbyshire Language Scheme, Detailed Test of Comprehension (Madislover, M. and Knowles, W. 1979)

Objective:	To ascertain the 'information load' the child can process in one presentation. To find out which types of words or structures are understood at different levels of information.
Age range:	Wide – designed for use with children with severe learning difficulties.
Equipment/Presentation:	Real objects and pictures are used. Child is asked to respond to questions and follow instructions, carefully controlled to ascertain precise areas of understanding.
Strengths:	Can be incorporated into play activities. Can be administered over several sessions. Gives good indications of language structures to work on.
Weaknesses:	Not standardised. Can be lengthy to administer. Must be trained to administer.
Type of result:	Qualitative – in terms of 'information carrying words' and grammatical structures.

Renfrew Action Picture Test (Renfrew, C. 1988)

Objectives	To elicit sample of spoken language that can be evaluated in terms of information given (i.e. naming objects, describing actions) and grammar used (i.e. use of tense endings, plurals).
Age range:	3.06–8.0 years.
Equipment/Presentation:	Tester presents 10 activity pictures one at a time. A standard question is asked (designed to elicit a specific structure) and the response written down.
Strengths:	Quick and easy to administer and core. Separates content and grammar.
Weaknesses:	Child with comprehension difficulties may lose marks if fails to respond to question appropriately, e.g. use wrong tense. The test elicits a fairly limited sample.
Type of results:	Age equivalent for information and grammar.

South Tyneside Assessment of Syntactic Structures (Armstrong, S. and Ainley 1988)

Objectives:	To elicit specific types of language structure, for syntactic analysis.
Age range:	3–7 years.
Equipment/Presentation:	Child is shown a series of cartoon-like pictures and asked a specific question about each one. The response is written down.
Strengths:	Children like the pictures. Fairly quick to administer.
Weaknesses:	Some of the questions contain implied information which some children misinterpret.
Type of results:	For more useful information the responses need to be analysed according to the LARSP procedure (Language Assessment, Remediation and Screening Procedure). This gives detailed information about the type of sentences, phrases, clauses and words used. LARSP describes stages of development, which can be linked to age levels.

South Tyneside Assessment of Phonology (STAP) (Armstrong, S. and Ainley, E. 1988)

Objectives:	To obtain single word responses; using most sounds of English and all positions in a word, e.g. 'b' in bed, table and web.
Age range:	Not standardised, but appeals to younger children.
Equipment/Presentation:	Child is shown cartoon-style pictures and asked to name them.
Strengths:	Easy to administer. Gives a broad sample to analyse.
Weaknesses:	Can be too long for 3 to 4-year-olds. Does not give sample of connected speech.
Type of result:	Therapist analyses. No age norms appropriate.

Test for Reception of Grammar (Bishop, D. V. M. 1989 2nd edn)

Objectives:	A test of auditory-verbal comprehension of syntax and morphological markers (e.g. plural 's'; word order).
Age range:	4–12 years.
Equipment/Presentation:	Child is shown a series of pages of four coloured drawings, and must point to the picture corresponding to the sentence given by the tester.

Strengths:	Children like the pictures. Quick and easy to administer. A range of results obtainable.
Weaknesses:	Does not test structures involving tense markers. Relies on reasonable auditory attention ability.
Type of result:	Age equivalent and percentile. Analysis of lexical or grammatical errors.

Test of Word Finding (German, D. 1986)

Objectives:	After determining that child knows a word, she/he is asked to 'retrieve' the word in different linguistic contexts to ascertain the presence and nature of a word finding difficulty.
Age range:	6–12 years.
Equipment/Presentation:	Child is asked to name pictures, complete sentences and respond to descriptions. Responses are scored for speech and accuracy. Notes are made of any self-cueing strategies such as gesture.
Strengths:	A thorough test which gives useful results.
Weaknesses:	American vocabulary and norms.
Type of result:	A profile of speech and accuracy in naming.

The Token Test (Di Simoni, E. 1978)

Objectives: instructions.	A test of language processing by following oral instructions.
Age range:	3–10 years.
Equipment/Presentation:	Child is presented with a set of tokens of different colours, shapes and size. Tester asks child to perform various actions with the tokens, increasing in linguistic complexity.
Strengths:	Children enjoy arranging the tokens. Quick to administer.
Weaknesses:	Failures may be due to poor knowledge of colour, shape and size labels, rather than language processing problems.
Type of results:	Scaled score.

Word Finding Vocabulary Scale (Renfrew, C. 1995)

Objective:	To assess expressive vocabulary.
Age range:	3–8 years.
Equipment/Presentation:	Child is asked to name 50 items (line drawings). If no response, tester tries to ascertain whether child does not recognise the picture, or does not know what it is called. Tester notes any prolonged pauses or errors.
Strengths:	Allows tester to note type of errors made and what sort of prompts help. Quick and easy to administer.
Weaknesses:	Does not allow detailed analysis of type of word-finding difficulty.
Type of result:	Age equivalent.

Interview schedule

Your recollections of the period of time when school placement was being sort out:

1. Before starting school

Before entry to school, what did you think that the educational provision might be for your child?

Were there any difficulties in securing the appropriate provision?

What are your recollections of this period?

2. Starting school

What was the provision for your child?

How did your child settle at school during this transition period?

What were the most difficult aspects of this period?

How did you deal with them?

Looking back, what do you remember most about this time?

3. Current provision (Language Unit)

Do you think the provision is meeting/met his/her needs?

How much time does your child spend in mainstream?

How effective is this provision?

4. Local mainstream school (post Language Unit)

What were your feelings when you heard that your child was ready to return or go to the local mainstream school in your area?

What are your recollections of the transition period?

How could it have been made better?

How welcome did you feel?

How quickly did your child settle?

What factors contributed to your child's settling?

Has your child encountered any difficulties subsequent to transfer?

5. The effects of communication impairments upon relationships

What effects have your child's difficulties had upon family relationships (not brothers and sisters)?

What effects have your child's difficulties had on their brothers and sisters?

What effects have your child's difficulties had upon relationships with friends?

6. In the light of your experiences to date, what would you say to professionals involved with language impaired children?

7. Similarly, what would you say to them about inclusion?

References

AFASIC Publications with the Speech and Language Therapy Department, Hounslow and Spelthorne Health Authority. *Listening Skills Part 1 (3–7), Part 2 (7–11)*.

Aitchison, J. (1996) *The Language Web. Reith Lecture*. BBC Publications.

Armstrong, S. and Ainley, M. (1988) *South Tyneside Assessment of Phonology* (STAP). Northumberland: STASS Publications.

Armstrong, S. and Ainley, M. (1988) *South Tyneside Assessment of Syntactic Structures*. Northumberland: STASS Publications.

Baker, L. and Cantwell, D. P. (1987) 'A prospective psychiatric follow-up of children with speech and language disorders', *Journal of the American Academy of Child Psychiatry* **26**, 546–53.

Bankson, N. W. (1990) *The Bankson Language Test*. London: The Psychological Corporation.

Barkley, R. A. (1997) *AD/HD and the Nature of Self-control*. Calif. USA: Guildford Press.

Beitchman, J. H. *et al.* (1986) 'Prevalence of psychiatric disorders in children with speech and language disorders', *Journal of the American Academy of Child and Adolescent Psychiatry* **25**, 528–35.

Berk, L. E. and Potts, M. K. (1991) 'Development and functional significance of private speech among AD/HD and normal boys', *Journal of Abnormal Child Psychology* **19**, 357–77.

Bishop, D. V. M. (1989) *Test of Reception for Grammar* (2nd edn) c/o Age Cognitive Performance Research Centre, University of Manchester M13 9PL.

Bishop, D. V. M. and Edmundson, A. (1987) 'Language-impaired four-year-olds: distinguishing transient from persistent impairment', *Journal of Speech and Hearing Disorders* **52**, 156–73.

Bishop, D. V. M. and Rosenbloom, L. (1987) 'Classification of childhood language disorders', in Yule W. and Rutter M. (eds) *Language Development and Disorders: Clinics and Developmental Medicine*, nos 101 and 102. London: MacKeith.

Bishop, D. V. M. (1994) 'Is specific language impairment a valued diagnostic category? Genetic and psycholinguistic evidence'. *Philosophical Transactions of the Royal Society*, **B** 346, 105–111.

Bishop, D. V. M., North T. and Donlan, C. (1996). 'Non word repetition as a behavioural marker for inherited language impairment: Evidence from a twin study'. *Journal of Child Psychology and Psychiatry*, **37**, 391–403.

Blackman, B. (1991) *Early Intervention for Children's Reading Problems: Clinical Applications of the Research in Phonological Awareness*.

Bloom, L. and Lahey, M. (1978) *Language Development and Language Disorders*. New York: Wiley.

Boehm, R. (1988) *Boehm Test of Basic Concepts (Revised)*. USA: Psychological Corporation/Harcourt Brace Jovanovich.

Boivin, M. and Begin, G. (1986) 'Temporal reliability and validity of three sociometric assessment with young children', *Canadian Journal of Behavioural Science* **18**, 167–72.'

Bradley, L. and Bryant, P. E. (1983) 'Categorising sounds and learning to read – a causal connection', *Nature* **301**, 409–521.

Bradley, L. and Bryant, P. E. (1985) *Children's Reading Problems*. Oxford: Blackwell.

Burgess, J. and Bransby, G. (1990) 'An evaluation of speech and language skills of children with EBD problems', *College of Speech and Language Therapy Bulletin* **453**.

Buzan, T. (1995) *Use Your Head*. London: BBC Books.

Byers-Brown, B. and Edwards, M. (1989) *Developmental Disorders of Language*. London: Whurr Publications.

Cerutti, D. T., (1989) 'Discrimination theory of rule-governed behaviour'. *Journal of the Experimental Analysis of Behaviour* **51**, 259–76.

Conti-Ramsden, G. and Botting, N. (1999a) 'Characteristics of children attending language units in England: a national study of 7 year olds', *International Journal of Language and Communication Disorders* **34**, 359–66.

Conti-Ramsden, G. and Botting, N. (1999b) 'Classification of children with specific language impairment', *Journal of Speech, Language and Hearing Research* **42**, 1195–204.

Cummins, J. (1986) *Empowering Minority Students: A Framework for Intervention*. Cambridge, Mass: Harvard University Press.

Daines, B., (1998) 'AFASIC Workshop for EPs' (unpublished course notes).

Daines, B. and Ripley, K. (1992) 'Reading and Signing' (unpublished study).

Daines, B. Fleming, P. and Miller, C. (1996) *Spotlight on Special Educational Needs: Speech and Language Difficulties*. Tamworth: NASEN.

Denham, S. A. (1992) 'Baby looks very sad: implications of conversations about feelings between mother and pre-schooler', *British Journal of Child Psychology*, **10**, 301–15.

Denham, S. A. *et al.* (1990) 'Emotional and Behavioural predictions of peer status in young pre-schoolers', *Child Development* **61**, 1145–52.

Di Simoni, E. (1978) *The Token Test*. London: The Psychological Corporation.

Dodge, K. A., (1996) 'A social information processing model of social competence in children', in Perlmulter, M. (ed.) *The Minnesota Symposium of Psychology*, 77–125. Hillsdale, NJ: Lawrence Erlbaum.

Donahue, M. *et al.* (1994) 'Links between language and emotional/ behavioural disorders', *Education and Treatment of Children* **17**, 244–54.

Dunn, J. and Brown, J. (1991) 'Family talk about feeling states and childrens' later understanding of others' emotions', *Developmental Psychology* **27**(3), 448–55.

Dunn, L. M., Whetton C. and Burley, J. (1997) *The British Picture Vocabulary Scale*, (2nd edn). Windsor: NFER/Nelson.

Education Department of Western Australia (1989a) *First Steps, Oral Language Development Continuum*. Rigby Heinnemann.

Education Department of Western Australia (1989b) *Oral Language Resource book*. Rigby Heinnemann.

Edwards, S. *et al.* (1997) *Reynell Developmental Language Scales III*,

University of Reading Edition. Windsor: NFER/Nelson.

DfEE (1997) *Excellence for All Children: Meeting Special Educational Needs*. London: The Stationery Office.

DfEE (1999) The National Numeracy Strategy. Sudbury: DfEE Publications.

Frith, U. (1989) *Autism: Explaining the Enigma*. Oxford: Blackwell.

Funk, J. B. and Ruppert, E. S. (1984) 'Language disorders and behavioural problems in pre-school children', *Journal of Developmental and Behavioural Paediatrics* **5**, 357–60.

Gordon, N. (1991) 'The relationships between language and behaviour', *Developmental Medicine and Child Neurology* **33**, 86–9.

Goswami, V. (1996) 'Rhyme and reading', *Child Education*, April, 16–17.

Hadley, M. and Rice, J. (1991) 'Predictions of interactional failure in pre-school children', *Journal of Speech, Language and Hearing Research* **34**, 1308–17.

ICAN, *Language Through Reading Programme*. London: ICAN Publications.

Johnson, D. W. *et al.* 'Effects of co-operative, competitive and individualistic goal structures on achievement: A meta analysis'. *Psychological Bulletin* **89**, 47–62.

Johnson, D. W. and Johnson, R. T. (1989). *Co-operation and Competition: Theory and Research*. Edina, MNs Interaction Book Company.

Kaufman, A. S. and Kaufman, N. L. (1983) *Kaufman Assessment Battery for Children*. American Guidance Service, UK Distributor NFER/Nelson.

La Vigna, G. W., Willis, T. J. and Donnellan, E. A. (1989) 'The role of positive programming in behavioural treatment', in Cipani, E. (ed.) *Behavioural Approaches to the Treatment of Aberrant Behaviour*. AAMD Monograph Series. Washington DC: American Association on Mental Deficiency.

Layton, L. *et al.* (1996) 'Phonological Awareness and the Pre-School Child'. Final Report to the DfEE. Birmingham: The University of Birmingham.

Lewis, M. and Wray, D. (1995) *Writing Frames*. Exeter Extending Literacy Project.

Lipsky, D. K. and Gartner, A. (1997) *Inclusion and School Reform: Transforming America's Classroom*. Baltimore: Paul. H. Brookes.

Locke, A. (1985) *Living Language*. Windsor: NFER/Nelson.

Locke, A. and Beech, M. (1992) *Teaching Talking*. Windsor: NFER/Nelson.

Madisiover, M. and Knowles, W. (1979) *Derbyshire Language Scheme, Detailed Test of Comprenhension*. Derbyshire County Council.

Milne, A. A. (1924) *When We Were Very Young*. London: Methuen Children's Books.

Neale, M. D. (1998) *Neale Analysis of Reading Ability*, 2nd GB revision. Windsor: NFER/Nelson.

Oakhill, J. and Yuill, N. (1991) 'The remediation of reading comprehension difficulties', in Snowling, M. and Thomson, M. (eds) *Dyslexia: Integrating Theory and Practice*. London: Whurr..

Oakhill, J. and Yuill, N. (1995) 'Learning to understand written language', in Funnell, E. and Stuart, M. (eds) *Learning to Read: Psychology in the Classroom*. Oxford: Blackwell.

Paul, R. (1991) 'Profiles of toddlers with slow expressive language development', *Topics in Language Disorders* **11**(4), 1–13.

Pease, A. (1997) *Body Language. How to read others' thoughts by their gestures*. London: Sheldon Press.

Rapin, I. and Allen, D. A. (1987) 'Developmental dysphasia and autism in pre-school children: characteristics and subtypes', in Martin, J. *et al.* (eds) *Proceedings of the first international symposium on specific speech and language disorders in children*, 20–35. London: AFASIC.

Renfrew, C. (1994) *The Renfrew Language Scales: The Bus Story* (2nd edn). Oxford: Winslow Press.

Renfrew, C. (1995) *The Renfrew Language Scales: Word Finding Vocabulary Test* (4th edn). Oxford: Winslow Press.

Renfrew, C. (1997) *The Renfrew Language Scales: Action Picture Test* (4th edn). Oxford: Winslow Press.

Reynell, J. (1976) *Developmental Language Scales*. Windsor: NFER Nelson.

Rickerby, S. and Lambert, S. (1994) *Listening Skills Key Stage 1, Levels 1 and 2*. Birmingham: The Questions Publishing Co.

Rinald, W. (1992) *Social Use of Language Programme*. Windsor: NFER/Nelson.

Rinaldi, W. (1998) *Language Concepts to Access Learning*. Published by Wendy Rinaldi, MRCSLT, 18 Dorking Road, Chilworth, Surrey GU4 8NR.

Roid, H. G. and Miller, L. J., (1997) *Leiter International Performance Scale – Revised*. Ill. USA: Stoelting Co.

Semel, E., Wing, E., Secord, W. (1987) *Clinical Evaluation of Language Fundamentals* (CELF-R). London: The Psychological Corporation.

Skinner, B. F. (1953) *Science and human behaviour*. New York: Macmillan.

Snow, C. (1972) Mother's speech to children learning language. *Child Development*, **43**, 549–66.

Spence, S. H. (1987) 'The relationship between social-cognitive skills and peer sociometric status', *British Journal of Developmental Psychology* **5**, 347–56.

Stackhouse, J. and Wells, B. (1997) *Children's Speech and Literacy Difficulties*. London: Whurr Publications.

Stevenson, J. *et al.* (1985) 'Behaviour problems and language abilities at three years and behavioural deviance at eight years', *Journal of Child Psychology and Psychiatry and Allied Disciplines* **26**(2), 215–30.

Toomey, M. M. (1994) *Teaching Kids of All Ages to Ask Questions*. Oxford: Winslow Press.

Topping, K. (1992) 'Co-operative learning and peer tutoring: An overview'. *The Psychologist: Bulletin of the British Psychological Society* (1992), **5**, 151–161.

Vallance, D. *et al.* (1999) 'Discourse deficits associated with psychiatric disorders and with language impairments in children', *Journal of Child Psychology and Psychiatry and Allied Disciplines* **40**, 693–705.

Vygotsky, L. S. (1962) *Thought and Language*. Cambridge, Mass: MIT Press.

Walden, T. A. and Field, T. M. (1990) 'Pre school children's social competence and production and discrimination of affective expressions', *British Journal of Developmental Psychology* **8**, 65–76.

Ward, S. (1992) 'The predictive validity and accuracy of a screening test for language delay and auditory perceptual disorder', *European Journal of Disorders of Communication* **27**, 55–72.

Webster, A. and McConnell, C. (1987) *Children with Speech and Language Difficulties*. London: Castle.

Webster, A. and Webster, V. (1990) *Profiles of Development: Speech & Language*. Avec Designs.

Williams, D. (1995) *Early Listening Skills*. Oxford: Winslow Press.

Yuill, N. and Oakhill, J. (1998) 'Effects of inference awareness training on poor reading comprehension', *Journal of Applied Cognitive Psychology* **2**, 33–45.

Index